ROUTEMASTER
BUS

1954 onwards (all marks)

First published in November 2011

Andrew Morgan has asserted his moral right to be identified as the author of this work.

A catalogue record for this book is available from the British Library

ISBN 978 1 84425 938 0

Library of Congress control no. 2011930598

Published by Haynes Publishing,
Sparkford, Yeovil, Somerset BA22 7JJ, UK
Tel: 01963 442030 Fax: 01963 440001
Int. tel: +44 1963 442030 Int. fax: +44 1963 440001
E-mail: sales@haynes.co.uk
Website: www.haynes.co.uk

Haynes North America Inc.
861 Lawrence Drive, Newbury Park, California 91320, USA

Printed in the USA by Odcombe Press LP,
1299 Bridgestone Parkway, La Vergne, TN 37086

COVER CUTAWAY: *John Lawson*

ROUTEMASTER
BUS

1954 onwards (all marks)

Enthusiasts' Manual

An insight into maintaining and operating the
iconic vehicle of the British transport network

Andrew Morgan

Contents

6 Preface

7 Introduction

8 The Routemaster story

Prototypes, development and production variants	10
Maintenance and overhaul	25
The 1970s	25
Aldenham and the works float	26
The beginning of the end and life after London	32
1990s developments	37
Renaissance and the end in London	40

46 Anatomy of the Routemaster

Subframes	48
Engine	49
Cooling system	54
Fuel system	55
Exhaust system	56
Transmission	56
Steering gear	60
Axles and suspension	60
Brake gear	62
Braking system	64
Electrical equipment	66
Alternator	67
Automatic gearbox equipment	67
Starter motor	68
Batteries	68
Lighting equipment	69
Destination lighting	70
Instruments and switches	71
Windscreen wiper	72
Wheels and tyres	72
Body	72
Upholstery	82
Route destinations	82
Paintwork and livery	82
Dimensions and weight	83

84 The owner's view

So who buys a Routemaster?	86
Buying a Routemaster	86
Running costs	88
Values	89
Researching the history	90
Limits to authenticity	90
Restoration	95
The Routemaster industry	100
Driving and handling	101
The inevitable paperwork	103

104 The mechanic's view

Recommended lubricants and fluids	106
Safety first	107
Tools and working facilities	107
Daily checks	107
Annual servicing	108
Maintenance	115
Obtaining spare parts	127

130 Routemaster in the 21st century

Where to find and ride on a Routemaster	131
Museums, rallies and running days	137

144 Epilogue: preserving Routemasters

150 Appendices

Appendix 1 – A selection of notable surviving Routemasters	150
Appendix 2 – How many roadworthy Routemasters survive worldwide?	154
Appendix 3 – Routemaster types	155
Appendix 4 – Routemaster codes	156
Appendix 5 – Glossary of terms and abbreviations	158
Appendix 6 – Useful contacts	160
Appendix 7 – Further reading	163

164 Index

OPPOSITE RM16 illustrates how easily access can be achieved to not only the main mechanical components, but to ancillary units as well. *(Mark Kehoe)*

Preface

BELOW Two RMs that have been restored to non-London liveries are Clydeside Scottish liveried RM835 and Kelvin Scottish liveried RM910. They are shown re-united, in April 2011 at Kirkby Stephen railway.
(Steve Fennell)

The story of the Routemaster is unique and incredible. It was the last bus to be designed by London Transport for service in London, and the fact that Routemasters can still be found in operational passenger service, not only in their home city but also around the world, is a tribute to this truly special vehicle. No other passenger-carrying vehicle has survived in operational service quite like the Routemaster. No other vehicle or mode of transport is remembered with such affection. Wherever the Routemaster operated or still operates, new friends are made; its drivers, conductors, mechanics, managers and enthusiasts instantly become admirers. To reach the milestone of 50 years in service in 2004 was an incredible achievement, but the story did not end there, and the legend has continued to grow.

The most successful motorbus ever designed? Probably – and in terms of economy of operation, longevity and fitness for purpose, then certainly.

Introduction

Fifty-seven years ago, at the Earls Court Commercial Motor Show on 24 September 1954, the first Routemaster, RM1, was revealed to the general public.

It was a design that was far ahead of its time, with a fully automatic gearbox, hydraulic brakes, independent front suspension, comfortable seating and – a rare feature in the 1950s – a heater. By using a light alloy body it was possible to produce a 64-seat bus within the weight limits of the older 56-seat RT bus. The Routemaster also differed from earlier London designs in being of integral construction, which means that instead of having a traditional body and chassis, the Routemaster has a strengthened body that doesn't require a chassis to take the stress, and the mechanical units are mounted on front and rear subframes rather than a heavy fixed chassis. When it went into production in the late 1950s it had power-assisted steering, and soon featured items such as air suspension and fluorescent lighting as standard fitments.

The Routemaster was the last bus to be wholly designed by London Transport. The first examples were intended to complete the replacement of the once large London trolleybus fleet. Built between 1958 and 1968, it was the last open-platform bus to enter service in the capital.

It was designed for a 17-year life and was intended to be replaced by 1985. Yet some 57 years after its first appearance, just under 700 examples of this popular and famous bus still exist in the British Isles, out of a total of 2,876 built. Even more remarkably, until the summer of 2003 almost 650 of these were still in operational use in the capital alone, though by the end of 2005 this total had reduced to just ten, with their only operational service being the city's two Heritage routes. It's also noteworthy that approximately 600 more examples survive in a further 59 countries.

Today, the Routemaster has justifiably become a legend.

Acknowledgements

A number of people and organisations assisted with the compilation of this manual, from vehicle owners to photographers, and between us we assembled sufficient material – and photographs in particular – to fill several books, not just one! However, the author would like to thank the following people and organisations in particular for their help: Allison Transmission, Tim Barrington, Cummins UK, Ensign Bus, Rob Duker, Mark Kehoe, John Keohane and Gavin Bishop from the South Devon Railway, Brian Lewer, Pete Rodgers, Phil Willson of the RM8 Club, and last but not least, my wife and family for their patience.

Warning

Whilst every attempt has been made throughout this book to emphasise the safety aspects of maintaining, restoring and driving Routemasters, the author and publishers accept no liability whatsoever for any damage, injury or loss resulting from the use of this book, nor any responsibility for any errors and omissions. Also, it should be noted that no single book on this subject will ever include sufficient information to resolve every potential problem.

ABOVE An overhauled B-frame is being re-assembled prior to fitting to RM121, which is shown undergoing refurbishment by Marshall Bus UK in 2001. *(Mark Kehoe)*

Chapter One

The Routemaster Story

The history of the Routemaster can be traced back to 1947, when within London Transport there had been various discussions concerning chassisless, lightweight vehicles being the future direction that bus design would follow. At the time, the production of the AEC Regent III – the famous 7½ft (2.29m) wide, 56-seat RT type – had recently recommenced following World War Two, and trams, trolleybuses and diesel-engined motorbuses were the three main types of public passenger transport on the capital's roads.

OPPOSITE Seen in the AEC works at Southall in July 1962 is a mixture of RMs and RMCs, as well as a handful of other 1960s commercials. Completed vehicles from Park Royal were driven to Southall prior to delivery to London Transport at Aldenham works. *(Geoff Rixon)*

It was late 1959 before full-scale introduction of the Routemaster into passenger service commenced, and nobody could have expected its lengthy design process to have created a bus of such longevity.

Prototypes, development and production variants

London Transport's ultimate aim was to construct a lightweight double-deck bus built of light alloy materials that would result in improved construction methods as well as a reduction in the amount of skilled labour required. The use of aluminium was revolutionary at the time; it was not adopted as standard for bus manufacture in the United Kingdom until the 1970s.

During World War Two, London Transport had gained a great deal of experience with aluminium alloy technology and a standardised parts system, as it had led the London Aircraft Production Group (LAP) consortium, based at factories in Aldenham and Leavesden, north of London in Hertfordshire. An impressive total of 700 Handley Page Halifax bombers had been assembled in the unused Underground depot at Aldenham. After the war the conversion of Aldenham Works back to its intended use as an Underground depot was never completed, and it was rebuilt as a bus overhaul works instead.

In 1951, A.A.M. ('Bill') Durrant – chief engineer (road services) for London Transport between 1945 and 1965 – produced a document entitled 'Development and General Specification – IM Vehicle', the letters IM standing for 'integrally mounted'. This provided the guidelines and agreed direction for the design of a new vehicle intended for service in London. It was to be of chassisless type (ie of integral construction using light alloy, with no wooden members), its basic dimensions were to be 27ft (8.23m) long, 8ft (2.44m) wide and 14ft 4½in (4.38m) high; and it was to have an improved suspension to give greater softness and a more comfortable ride. This last point was the answer to two requirements: firstly to extend the life of the vehicle's structure, and secondly – and more importantly – to compete with the motor cars that were now taking large numbers of potential passengers away from the bus operators. At the time there was still an aspiration to reduce running costs by cutting the overall weight, thereby improving fuel consumption and cutting fuel costs. It was realised that not only did a reduction in weight reduce such costs, but it also had an effect on the wear of brakes and thus the service life of the vehicle as a whole.

If one remembers that a bus doesn't carry a full load of passengers all day, there's a direct saving of fuel costs when a bus is just carrying empty seats. In fact the basic Routemaster was lighter than its predecessor, the 7½-ton RT, yet carried eight more passengers, so one can instantly see the logic behind this aspiration to save weight in reduced costs per passenger. The extra passengers were to be accommodated by careful respacing of the seats and by the addition of a foot (0.3m) to the vehicle's length; thus a bus that was only 5% longer had 14% more seats.

From 1951 AEC became involved in the project, and in 1952 they commenced development of the IM. At this stage they were preparing their proposals based purely on the design requirements that had been set by London Transport for the engine, transmission, suspension and braking systems, which were to be mounted in an integral aluminium structure. To achieve the increase in seating capacity the lower saloon passenger area was increased to its maximum and the unusual solution was adopted of locating the radiator and fan under the driver. The design for the suspension was fully independent front and rear, using traditional wishbones with coil springs. At the rear, substantial wishbones and the differential were to be mounted directly on to the bodywork. AEC simplified the design, using a conventional one-piece axle with redesigned differential, and long parallel radius arms that became what we would now recognise as the rear subframe.

The IM design called for an hydraulically operated gearbox system; this had been chosen to sit alongside the proposed hydraulic braking system. The commonly used air brakes were to be abandoned in favour of a hydraulic system that used a mineral oil, the idea being to eliminate any delay in air brake systems by using a continually running pump and hydraulic brake accumulators. (The theory was that a substantially reduced braking distance would be possible compared to air brakes, but in reality this was not seen, as drivers became confident with the new system and generally drove to their own or the vehicle's limit.)

This was the basis on which the detailed design was undertaken by AEC. The hydraulic gearbox was reviewed and AEC were unable to verify any advantages in unit life or performance, but could see additional cost and manufacturing complications. Thus they concluded that the air-operated gearbox should be retained, and the vehicle ended up having an air system and a hydraulic system fitted. The traditional mechanical handbrake was retained, although its position was moved inboard of the driver rather than being located in an outside position as fitted to the RT types.

Following the completion of the running gear design, AEC produced two prototype sets that were delivered to London Transport's Chiswick Works for assembly within the prototype bodyshells during 1953. Extensive service trials had already been undertaken with the existing RT fleet prior to the construction of the new vehicles – for example, from late 1948 early examples of vehicles fitted with automatic gearboxes and hydraulic power braking were run in daily service in London.

In 1952, Douglas Scott, from the industrial design partnership Scott Ashford Associates, was commissioned to assist with the design of the IM's bodywork. Externally he designed the curves that turned the essentially square box into the Routemaster. A full-size mock-up was made to finalise the frontal treatment, numerous alterations were undertaken, and the results appeared in 1954, when the first example of the new bus was unveiled. The front, and in particular the bonnet, were the main areas that changed during this time. These had been originally designed by A.B.B. Valentine, but were redesigned in a neater form by Scott. The mock-ups latterly featured reduced destination displays compared with the RT, and this continued up to the completion of the first two prototypes, primarily due to the ongoing goal of reducing unnecessary weight.

Internally too Douglas Scott had his say in the final design. Although some of his ideas,

such as fibreglass seat frames and fluorescent lights, were rejected, his colour scheme of 'Sung' yellow ceilings and the design for the seat moquette made it into production. This seat moquette, in a pattern of red, yellow and turquoise, was very hard-wearing, and even after several years' heavy use the pattern remained clear. In addition Scott designed the space under the stairs for the conductor; this increased the platform area, and also doubled as a space for the conductor to stand out of the way of boarding and alighting passengers. Scott also provided input for the third and fourth prototypes in 1955, and in the final design for the production vehicles as signed off in 1956.

Park Royal Vehicles, based in London NW10, was a sister company of AEC within the Associated Commercial Vehicles group. After World War Two it had produced some 3,000 bodies for the RT family of vehicles and was an obvious choice for the IM project. From early 1953, therefore, it commenced detailed design of the bodywork for the prototypes. This was based not only on the IM design but also on jig-built construction methods, and as with the mechanical elements utilised standardisation of units to achieve parts interchangeability in order to minimise time spent off the road undergoing maintenance or repairs. The production of the first prototype was started later the same year.

It should be remembered that with this integral vehicle, the IM, there was no chassis. The aluminium bodywork supported the main mechanical units in two subframes, and the remaining mechanical units were fixed directly to the bodywork. Thus the bodywork is the majority of the bus, so perhaps the final vehicle should have been called the Park Royal Routemaster and not the AEC Routemaster! This would have made a great deal of sense, as later in its production life there was an alternative engine supplier, and from the late 1980s onwards a variety of different engine types were fitted.

It had become known on 28 April 1954 that the replacement of London Transport's trolleybus fleet was to commence from 1957. At the same time it was announced that the replacement vehicle would be of a lightweight type and would be under test by the end of 1954.

RIGHT RM1
immediately prior
to being unveiled to
the general public
in September 1954.
Minus its front panel,
it reveals the
engine, the front
crossmember and
the lack of a radiator.
(London Transport)

A total of four prototypes were completed between 1954 and 1957. The first two were assembled at the now demolished London Transport works at Chiswick, although in close cooperation with AEC at nearby Southall and coach-makers Park Royal Vehicles. For the other two prototypes London Transport chose two separate companies, although Leyland supplied the mechanical equipment for both. These prototypes had bodywork built respectively by Weymann at Addlestone and Eastern Coach Works at Lowestoft, the vehicle produced by the latter being an experimental double-deck Green Line coach.

The first prototype was unveiled on the AEC stand at the Earls Court Commercial Motor Exhibition on 24 September 1954, where it was the star attraction. Here it was identified as the 'Routemaster' for the first time, and numbered as RM1. Its weight at this time was 6 tons 14 cwt 2 qtrs (6.833 tonnes), which was, impressively, just over three-quarters of a ton lighter than the standard RT.

When first shown to the general public, RM1 was fitted with an AEC A204 9.6-litre engine, in similar format to the RT, but this was only a temporary fitment pending completion of the

development of a new unit. To the rear of the engine was fitted a fluid flywheel. The gearbox was an epicyclic type and was mounted amidships, but with no chassis it was fitted directly to the underside of the bodywork. As tested on RTs, this was an hydraulically operated unit controlled by a column-mounted gear lever with no clutch or operating pedal. The radiator was fitted under the floor behind the engine and had a chain-driven fan. This unusual feature was necessary to keep the total length of the vehicle below 27ft, and to allow the largest area possible for passenger seating.

The standard leaf springs of previous buses were replaced by coils (vertical steel springs) with shock absorbers; this provided the excellent ride characteristics that, over 50 years later, are still very comfortable and acceptable. The rear axle, as fitted to the rear subframe, was to a spiral bevel drive rather than the more familiar worm and wheel type. Rather than a full air-brake system as fitted on previous London buses, a power hydraulic system was fitted. As well as saving weight this had other advantages, such as not being susceptible to freezing or corrosion. The system was powered by an hydraulic pump mounted to the front of the

gearbox, which fed two pressure accumulators mounted under the floor. RM1 was built with conventional worm and nut steering gear. The bodywork was built from aluminium with some fibreglass panels but little or no timber.

In 1955 an extensive stress measurement and strain-gauge programme was undertaken with the first two prototypes at the MIRA test centre at Nuneaton, with AEC interested in the independent front suspension crossmember and parts of the rear radius arms, and Park Royal interested in the bodywork. Later the same year they were dispatched for further tests to the Ministry of Supply's Fighting Vehicle Proving Ground at Chobham test track in Surrey.

For a double-decker, the ride quality and stability were immediately noticeable as being far better than anything else available at the time. The Routemaster's success can be partly attributed to its ride, which has maintained its class-leading qualities throughout its operational life.

Following trials RM1 underwent various modifications, including the installation of a more familiar layout of destination equipment and the fitment of saloon heating and a ventilation system. To enable the latter to work,

the now familiar grille was fitted below the front destination boxes on the line of the relief band, and an additional radiator (or heat exchanger) was fitted behind it. The opening front windows on both decks were removed and various air outlets were fitted at the front of each saloon. Combined together all these modifications increased the weight of the vehicle to 6 tons 17 cwt (6.960 tonnes).

Following these alterations RM1 was licensed for passenger service on 11 January 1956 and was initially used for driver training, before entering service on route 2 (Golders Green to Crystal Palace) on 8 February from Cricklewood garage. It remained there for six months before returning to Chiswick Works for further modification, which included moving the radiator from its abortive underslung position to the front of the engine.

During July 1956 the Metropolitan Police authorised an increase in maximum vehicle length to 30ft (9.15m); this was the reason why the radiator was moved and the grille assembly was modified accordingly. Along with this new radiator, the filler and header tank was then installed above the top of the radiator rather than on the front bulkhead. With this element of

ABOVE RM1 as it entered passenger service, by which time various modifications had been undertaken including fitment of a full destination display in keeping with the comprehensive information displayed on all London buses. The four prototypes were unique in that their fuel tanks were fitted on the nearside, whereas on production models this was switched to the offside. *(Alan Cross)*

the design finalised the appearance of the front – including the radiator grille, headlamp wings and bonnet – was updated, and a new-style protruding grille was fitted in front of the radiator. Overall length was now 27ft 4in (8.34m).

The opportunity was also taken to fit the latest type of AEC 9.6-litre engine; this was the unit that would become the AV590 and would become standard fitment for the majority of all production Routemasters. This further modification work took the vehicle's weight up to 7 tons 5 cwt (7.366 tonnes), which was the weight that the standard RM would remain throughout production.

Following the service trials of RM1 in 1956 complaints were received of heavy steering. Consequently when it came to production vehicles, power assistance was fitted to the steering system, but not full power steering.

RM1 then re-entered passenger service from Cricklewood garage on 6 March 1957, where it saw use on route 260 (Monday to Saturdays) and route 2 (Sundays), and remained in service until 31 July 1959. It was subsequently overhauled and only saw use as a driver trainer thereafter until withdrawal in October 1972. It was repainted in February 1964, when

the opportunity was taken to fit a standard production-style bonnet, radiator grille, nearside wing assembly and headlamp panels.

The second prototype, RM2, was also assembled at Chiswick Works and followed after RM1. It was taken into stock on 10 March 1955 and immediately commenced a series of tests and trials. It remained in grey primer, and had been fitted with a smaller 7.68-litre AV470 engine complete with front-mounted radiator for these trials. Numerous modifications were carried out before it eventually entered service, including a revised radiator fitment with the larger 9.6-litre engine, power assistance for the steering, a fully automatic gearbox and a heating system. The change to a larger engine proved London Transport's belief that a de-rated large engine is preferable to a smaller engine being made to work harder; not only does the larger engine produce a more economical result, but it lasts longer and provides better performance without being over-stretched. The additional 6cwt (50.8kg) weight disadvantage was decided to be a sacrifice worth making.

Internally RM2 had grey plastic window surrounds in lieu of the red rexine on RM1, which had the effect of lightening the interior. This new feature was later to be included in the production vehicles.

RM2 was then painted in country area green livery and, after further tests, entered passenger service from Reigate garage on 20 May 1957 on routes 406 and 406A (Redhill to Kingston). However, its days in service were few and after various problems, notably with the transmission, it was returned to Chiswick Works on 8 August and repainted red. It re-entered passenger service on 18 September from Turnham Green garage on route 91 (Monday to Saturday) and route 27 (Sundays). This location was a common choice for experimental vehicles as it was the closest operational garage to the experimental department at Chiswick Works.

Subsequently RM2 returned to Chiswick at various times on a regular basis, and in February 1958 the decision was made not only to change the gearbox from an hydraulically-operated Self-Changing Gears unit to an electro-pneumatic D182 unit, but also to fit Dunlop air suspension for the first time, along with the necessary compressor.

BELOW RM2 entered passenger service over a year after RM1, and in country area green livery. This posed photograph at Epsom shows the new-style grille that was fitted in lieu of the original flat front; this became necessary after the radiator was moved to its traditional position at the front of the vehicle.
(London Transport)

RM2 then continued in passenger service from 1 July 1958 to 1 November 1959, when it was demoted to training duties until withdrawal in 1972. It was repainted in January 1964, when, as with RM1, the opportunity was taken to fit a standard bonnet, radiator grille, nearside wing assembly and headlamp panels.

The third prototype, RM3, was initially numbered RML3 and was the last of the four prototypes to be finished. The bodywork was completed by Weymann, part of the Metro Cammell Weymann (MCW) group, at their Addlestone works in Surrey. London Transport had a policy of sourcing large contracts from several competing companies. Therefore alternative suppliers were investigated as part of the Routemaster programme, which is why the order for RML3 went to MCW. Furthermore, instead of the mechanical units being supplied by AEC, for this vehicle they were supplied by Leyland Motors Limited, with a 9.8-litre Leyland 0600 engine being fitted from new. The Wilson-type electro-hydraulic gearbox from Self-Changing Gears was fitted operating in fully automatic mode. The steering was provided with power assistance, but of a different type to that on the other prototypes, and a hydraulic braking system was fitted, this time supplied by Clayton Dewandre.

RML3's bodywork was nearer the final production specification and featured numerous amendments, including a neater flush-fitting grille below the front destination blind box, direction indicators fitted vertically rather than horizontally at the rear, improved detailing around the front upper deck windows, and conventional aluminium beading or mouldings as cover plates across the bodywork panels. A narrower side-lifting bonnet was also fitted, as were a different nearside wing assembly and headlamp panels. The radiator grille was to the same design as carried by RM2 when it entered service in 1957. Additionally, the wheelbase was 16ft 10in (5.13m), which was an inch longer than RM1 and RM2. Internally, the window surrounds were again grey, although this was now called 'Chinese green' and matched the rear of the seat backs. The seat frames were to a new design and were of chromium-plated lightweight steel rather than polished alloy. Unladen vehicle weight was 7 tons 5 cwt

(7.366 tonnes), the same as the rebuilt first two prototypes.

RML3 was officially delivered in July 1957. After trials by Leyland in Lancashire, and driver training, in January 1958 it entered service from Willesden garage on route 8 (Wembley to Old Ford) Mondays to Saturdays and route 8B on Sundays. However, its days in passenger service were short-lived and from November 1959 it became a driver trainer. Its use in this capacity was nevertheless somewhat spasmodic and it was overhauled in 1965 before being put back on the road after a considerable period out of use. At this overhaul the opportunity was taken to fit a standard bonnet, radiator grille, nearside wing assembly and headlamp panels, which made it the last of the prototypes to retain its original style. In September 1961 the fleet number designation RML was amended to RM, and this corresponded with the delivery of the first 30ft (9.15m) Routemasters, which then inherited the RML designation.

The fourth and final prototype, numbered CRL4, was an experimental Green Line coach, and like RML3 its mechanical units were supplied by Leyland. The Green Line network

BELOW **The third Routemaster was numerically the first to be constructed with a Leyland engine, and its fleet number was initially RML3 in consequence (the 'L' standing for Leyland). Although it was built with an alternative frontal design, both externally and internally, the bodywork closely resembled production examples.**

(London Transport)

was at this time a series of limited-stop express routes operated by single-deck AEC Regal IV buses equipped as coaches.

The bodywork for CRL4 was built by Eastern Coach Works (ECW) at Lowestoft. Although they were part of the British Transport Commission it was unusual for this company to complete vehicles for London Transport, and it's therefore surprising that they completed one of the prototype Routemasters.

As with RML3, CRL4 externally resembled the production Routemasters, although it was finished to a higher standard for its Green Line duties. Platform doors were fitted, so an emergency exit was incorporated on the rear elevation of the bodywork. From an appearance point of view, mouldings were fitted around the windows and painted pale green, a raised bullseye motif was fitted on each side, and polished trim was fitted to the lights and front wheels. A pale cream relief band was applied to the standard Green Line livery of Lincoln green, and the finished result was a very smart vehicle.

Other detail differences between this and the previous prototypes included, externally, the revised position of the offside route number box, the omission of the route number box under the front canopy, the revised position of the nearside route blind box (due to the platform doors), and a bonnet that opened from the front rather than sideways as on RML3. Initially the radiator grille didn't have a vertical central bar, but this was modified before CRL4 entered service. Internally it was finished to coach standards, with deeper padded seats and Green Line moquette. Luggage racks were fitted above the seats and the flooring was finished with a flat covering, without the usual slats along the gangway.

By early July 1957 the seating capacity had been reduced by three, as the bench seats across the rear wheels were uniquely replaced with two individual seats on the nearside and one on the offside.

The mechanical units fitted to CRL4 were the Leyland 0600 9.8-litre engine, and fully independent front suspension with long torsion bars and shock absorbers mounted between the wishbones, all in lieu of the previous set-up. At the rear standard coil springs were fitted. The redesign of the front suspension was carried out by Leyland to reduce roll and to suit the

longer, faster running of Green Line operations. A Self-Changing Gears RV35 electro-hydraulic gearbox was fitted, although it had become known by this stage that the electro-pneumatic type would be fitted in production vehicles. The fitted gearbox was fully automatic, with a manual override for second and third gears. First gear could only be selected manually and was not available when in fully automatic mode, as it was normally only used for pulling away on hills. Power-assisted steering wasn't fitted as the linkage was identical to that fitted to RM1.

At 7 tons 10 cwt (7.620 tonnes), this was now the heaviest Routemaster, and was equivalent to the weight of the RT but lighter than the 39-seat single-deck RF type (which was 7 tons 17 cwt, or 7.976 tonnes) and considerably lighter than subsequent replacement buses and coaches.

CRL4 was delivered on 14 June 1957, and after driver training and modifications entered passenger service on 9 October 1957 from Romford garage on route 721 (Aldgate to Brentwood). After a successful few months in service, CRL4 was moved to Reigate garage in January 1958. In May of the same year it was withdrawn for modifications, including the fitment of power-assisted steering, an electro-pneumatic AEC D182 gearbox and air suspension at the rear. From now onwards CRL4 continued trials on a number of routes with regular transfers to different garages.

In August 1961 CRL4 was reclassified as RMC4 in readiness for the production RMCs to be delivered in the summer of 1962, and in April 1962 the unique single seats were removed and standard longitudinal bench seats were installed over the rear wheels. With the delivery of the production RMCs, RMC4 – although quite different in a number of ways – was subsequently treated as a standard RMC vehicle.

RMC4 was overhauled in 1964 and, as with the other prototypes, the opportunity was taken to fit a standard bonnet, radiator grille and nearside wing assembly. However, the headlamp panels then fitted were of a later type, as previously trial-fitted to RMC1469, with dual headlamps (as fitted to the production RMCs and later adopted for the RCL and RMA classes). Also, the three-piece front destination blind boxes remained, the opportunity not

being taken to replace them with the two-piece design adopted for the production RMCs.

In the summer of 1958 two 'slave rigs' were built so that evaluation running could take place. (It had been hoped that production vehicles would be available by this time, but it was still some months before the first completed Routemasters were due to be delivered.) These slave rigs – lorry-like vehicles with half-cab bodies fitted to Routemaster mechanical units – were tested by being driven behind standard service buses to simulate operational running as closely as possible. Much valuable information was generated by these, and in 1960, with production now under way, the mechanical units from the slave rigs were transferred to vehicles then being built.

Although still unproven at this stage, the go-ahead for Routemaster production was given in 1956, initially for 850 vehicles, with delivery planned to commence in 1958. London Transport had an agreement whereby at least

75% of all new vehicles would be sourced from AEC and fellow member of the Associated Commercial Vehicles Group, Park Royal Vehicles. Following a tender process competing against two other companies, Park Royal was awarded the contract to build the bodies for the initial batch of production vehicles. The fact that other manufacturers were at the time building RML3 and CRL4 didn't change this decision. With long lead times to set up the required production lines, it necessitated a large order to be placed in order to benefit from the economies of scale.

With this formality complete, production commenced in 1958, although only one vehicle was finished during this year and bulk delivery did not start until May 1959. The Routemaster's contribution to the trolleybus replacement programme commenced later the same year.

Because it had originally been intended that there should be three slave rigs, the first production Routemaster to be delivered was numbered RM8. However, this wasn't actually

ABOVE As with RML3, the final of the four prototypes was fitted with a Leyland engine and its fleet number was initially CRL4 (rather than RM or RML4), which stood for 'Coach Routemaster Leyland'. This smart vehicle was the second to be painted in green livery, and as well as having various bodywork embellishments for its particular task it was the first Routemaster to be fitted with doors to the rear platform.

(London Transport)

ABOVE RM8 was a pre-production vehicle, delivered over six months ahead of the start of main production, but it mirrored the form followed by subsequent production models. *(RM8 Club)*

the first vehicle off the Park Royal production line, as it was hand-built ahead of the main batch for display on the Park Royal stand at the 1958 Commercial Motor Show. RM8 was then used for experimental purposes and wasn't officially taken into stock until March 1961, and even then didn't enter passenger service until March 1976, as it was retained at Chiswick Works for experimental purposes.

The first production vehicle was delivered on 11 May 1959, and by the end of the year production was running at around nine per week. The production vehicles closely resembled RML3, but with the final design of bonnet, radiator grille and nearside wing

ABOVE RM8 was displayed by Park Royal at the 1958 Commercial Motor Show and was then allocated to the experimental department of Chiswick Works. In 1975 it was replaced in this role by RM1368, and after overhaul at Aldenham Works it entered service from Sidcup garage in March 1976. In 1980 it was adopted as a garage Showbus and was then sold in May 1985, initially to the garage sports and social club and then to the RM8 Club for preservation. *(RM8 Club)*

assembly; the bonnet now opened from the front, with the hinges at the rear on the front bulkhead. One new feature of the production

RIGHT Three new front subframes from Southall undergoing inspection at Park Royal Vehicles prior to installation. Although they're complete a few notable items have yet to be changed, including the fitment of AEC-badged hubcaps to the wheel centres. The fitment of a radiator shield between early November and late March was customary before antifreeze came into widespread use.
(Author's collection)

ABOVE The construction of the lower deck of an RML body is well under way, with the crossmembers installed first followed by the side frames and then the mechanical units. The Park Royal Routemaster production line was, at the time, far ahead of similar factories; preassembled components were installed on jigs, thereby guaranteeing compatibility and consistent positioning of parts during replacement. *(Author's collection)*

BELOW The completed upper deck, fully glazed and partially painted, is then lifted across and fitted to the waiting lower deck. The final framings at each end, lower deck windows, floor finishings and electrical components are then completed prior to finishing the paintwork. Surprisingly the paintwork was applied by hand rather than being sprayed. *(Author's collection)*

LEFT The upper deck was constructed on a separate production line in a similar manner to the lower deck. The jig can be clearly seen here; the upper-deck floor for an RML has been assembled complete with the wiring for the lower-deck ceiling lighting units, prior to the side frames being attached. One of the side frames can be seen leaning against the completed upper deck in front. *(Author's collection)*

vehicles was brake-cooling grilles immediately below and inboard of the headlights. A neater design of radiator grille was also fitted, with stainless steel trim around the perimeter and the registration plate at the bottom. Mounted on the front of the bonnet in line with the centre of the radiator grille was a bullseye badge. Internally too the production vehicles matched RML3, and retained tungsten lighting with exposed bulbs.

After five years of trials the majority of the production vehicles were manufactured with the following key mechanical components:

- AEC AV590 9.6-litre six-cylinder engine.
- Electro-pneumatic AEC D182 gearbox with air compressor mounted to the front and driven by belts.
- Continuous-flow hydraulic braking system.
- Hydraulic power-assisted steering.
- Coil suspension front and rear.
- Spiral bevel-type differential with a ratio of 5.22:1.

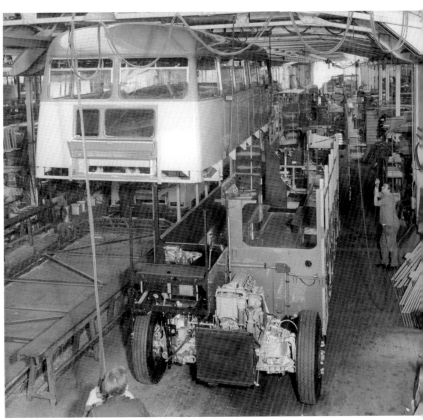

LEFT 11 November 1959 saw the implementation of stage four of the Trolleybus replacement programme, and was the first time that Routemasters became involved. Early vehicles that had been used for trials were delicensed and the full-scale introduction of Routemasters commenced. RM127 entered service the following month and is seen here at St Paul's, on one of the new routes, still in pristine original condition. The first 250 production RMs were all built with non-opening front upper-deck windows. *(Author's collection)*

Following on from the four prototypes, 2,871 production vehicles were built by AEC at Southall and Park Royal Vehicles. The basic model was 27ft 6in (8.39m) long, but this was just the first of six main variants and numerous minor modifications that took place during the production of the fleet. During 1962–63, 575 RMs were fitted with Leyland 9.8-litre 0600 engines from new, while from 1964 several batches were built with offside illuminated advert panels. Other design changes affected the radiator grille, headlamp panels, heater grille, offside route number panel, brake-cooling grilles and upper-deck front windows, to mention just a few examples. Nor does this list include the many mechanical component variations, or changes to the interior of the vehicle. What may appear to be a standard bus is actually far from it!

In 1961, 24 vehicles were built and then lengthened by the insertion of an additional 2ft 6in (0.76m) bay in the centre of their bodywork. Initially classified ER (for Extended Routemaster), and then reclassified RML, it surprisingly took until 1965 for this version with its 72-seat bodywork to become the standard product, but in the latter years of Routemaster service the RML was the most common type to be seen in London. The final Routemasters to be delivered, in February 1968, were the last of the 524-strong RML fleet. At approximately 7 tons 15 cwt (7.874 tonnes), the RML is still

RIGHT This spring 1962 view shows completed vehicles almost ready for delivery to London Transport. In the background are vehicles ready for the paint shop and completion of their topcoat. It can just been seen that the outer rear wheels haven't been fitted yet, and that the ticket bin on the platform is now finished in black rather than red as for the earlier vehicles.

(Fred Ivey)

LEFT 20 July 1960 saw the implementation of stage seven of the Trolleybus replacement programme; RM369 was one of a batch of vehicles to enter service at Shepherd's Bush garage on replacement routes 220 and 268. It is seen passing Trolleybus 1144 – the new order passing the old. *(Fred Ivey)*

RIGHT May 1963 sees Leyland-engined RM1603 standing outside the works at Southall; it entered passenger service the following month from Rye Lane garage, where it displaced older examples that were used to convert route 81B from RT operation. From RM949 onwards the radiator grille trim was changed from polished aluminium to stainless steel and included a vertical strip for the first time, but for now the roundel on the bonnet was retained. *(Colin Brown)*

BELOW The final batch of 500 RMLs was split, with 100 green country area and 400 red central area examples. Underlined gold fleet names were applied until the end of production, but the relief band was now flake grey in colour rather than cream. These four, seen at AEC works at Southall, were re-registered as SMK---F prior to entering service at the end of 1967. *(Fred Ivey)*

ABOVE Operating from Cricklewood garage, RM1043 was new into service in January 1962 and is seen here under the soon-to-be-demolished Trolleybus wires at North Acton. *(Fred W. Ivey)*

LEFT RM1292 and RMC1456 inside the finishing shop at the AEC works at Southall in July 1962. With the Trolleybus replacement programme completed on 9 May 1962, RM1292 entered service at Tottenham garage in December 1962 for route 73, as part of the first conversion of routes from RT operation. In August 1962 routes 715 and 715A saw the first batch of RMCs enter service, including RMC1456. Interestingly both survive to this day. *(Geoff Rixon)*

over four tonnes lighter than modern double-deck vehicles of similar passenger capacity.

Following on from the fourth prototype, 68 similar vehicles were built in 1962 for use on Green Line routes. This batch, classified RMC (Routemaster Coach), was built as 57-seaters, with fully-enclosed platforms, electrically-operated doors, fluorescent lighting, different interior trim, luggage racks and twin headlamps. Air suspension and fluorescent lighting were new ideas for the 1960s. In 1965, 43 further Green Line coaches were built to RML length (30ft), and classified as RCLs. These were 65-seaters and were equipped

LEFT Although it was nearly four years old, RMC1500 was still in original condition when seen at an empty Marble Arch in August 1966. We catch up with this vehicle in Chapter 5. *(Geoff Rixon)*

ABOVE New RCLs 2233, 2229 and 2225 seen at Park Royal in May 1965 prior to delivery. They included a number of features not previously seen, among them a new radiator grille incorporating a country area green triangular badge; the registration plate hanging below the radiator grille; headlamp panels without indents for the brake cooling grilles; two-piece front destination display; and a London Transport gold roundel (in lieu of the Green Line roundel mounted in the centre of the advert panels on the RMCs). The general view was that these changes, together with the continuous relief band across the heater grille below the blind box, produced a neater frontal appearance. *(Colin Brown)*

with larger AEC AV690 11.3-litre engines in lieu of the standard AEC AV590 9.6-litre unit. This was probably the most luxurious batch of Routemasters to be built.

A new variation of Routemaster was exhibited on the Park Royal stand at the Commercial Motor Show in October 1962. RMF1254, as it was numbered, was a front-entrance Routemaster with a front staircase, and was built to RML length. However, in line with many similar models available from its competitors the entrance was actually behind the front axle, so that this was really a forward-entrance vehicle rather than a front-entrance vehicle of the type that was just beginning to become standard for one-person operation. Nevertheless, with the driver being adjacent to the entrance there was still the potential for him to collect fares as passengers boarded, so that in principle this vehicle could also be operated by one person.

The bodywork was constructed from standard Routemaster parts. It was fitted with 69 seats and had an offside emergency exit behind the rear axle. One of the minor modifications to its trim involved the omission of the bonnet badge and the inclusion of a traditional-style AEC triangular badge on the radiator grille, but incorporating a London Transport bullseye. Mechanically it was fitted with standard AEC AV590 9.6-litre engine, as per the standard RML, and weighed 7 tons 14 cwt 2 qtrs (7.849 tonnes). It was used as a demonstrator to other potential operators in the Liverpool, Canterbury and, later, Halifax areas, and was only used in London on the British European Airways (BEA) service to Heathrow Airport. After a trial alongside RM8, RMF1254 was used with a trailer to carry luggage and continued with BEA for over two years.

Although sales to operators outside London were hoped for, the Routemaster's selling price was just too high compared with other vehicles available at the time, such as the Leyland Atlantean, and in hindsight even the long life and durability of the design weren't sufficient to compensate for the initial high costs. (The price of the front-engined Routemaster was reported to be approximately 12½% greater than the newer, rear-engined Atlantean.) Ironically, the only order for the Routemaster from outside London came from a company that had not actually tried out the demonstrator, namely Northern General of Gateshead, which from May 1964 took delivery of 50 vehicles of RML length, fitted with Leyland O600 9.8-litre engines and a forward staircase and entrance, as per RMF1254. With different opening windows and

ABOVE The first batch of vehicles for an operator outside London was delivered to Northern General at Gateshead between March and May 1964. Although constructed alongside some of the last London Routemasters with such features, the first batch of 18 Northern General vehicles retained their brake-cooling grilles and full-depth heater grille. However, the second batch, which followed between October 1964 and March 1965, had the later-style headlamp panels with indents for the brake cooling grilles, and a radiator grille that incorporated the registration plate, but with the relief band continuing across the heater grille. From RM2063, numerically, the relief band was continued across the heater grille. *(Maurice Bateman)*

interiors and many other features they were quite distinct from London examples.

BEA was the only other customer for the Routemaster, a batch of 65 vehicles being built for them in 1966–67. These were 27ft 6in (8.39m) 56-seaters, and were used to replace the company's AEC Regal 1½-deck coaches. Like the Northern General examples, they were forward-entrance and had different-style interiors, but mechanically they were fitted with the larger AEC AV690 11.3-litre engine and had air suspension. They were delivered in BEA blue and white livery, and towed luggage trailers.

There is one final footnote to the Routemaster story: the tale of what might have been. There was only one example, so it doesn't technically qualify for inclusion in this book, as you're never likely to own one, but for completeness' sake this unique vehicle can't be overlooked.

In 1966 a final prototype was completed. This was FRM1, a front-entrance, rear-engined Routemaster. It was built 60% from standard RM parts, with an AEC AV691 11.3-litre engine fitted transversely at the rear, and staircase and platform doors fitted at the front. This was the first integrally constructed, rear-engined

BELOW The only other customer for the Routemaster was British European Airways, for its service to Heathrow Airport from the West London Air Terminal at Gloucester Road. Passengers would hand over their luggage when they checked in at the Terminal and would then travel to Heathrow by bus, while their luggage was transported in the towed trailer. However, at the time the Ministry of Transport wouldn't allow 30ft vehicles with trailers, so the Park Royal production line had to revert to the shorter Routemaster variant. It was December 1977 before a railway (the Piccadilly Line underground extension) reached Heathrow airport. *(Geoff Rixon)*

BELOW In 1969 the BEA image was updated and their Routemasters were repainted from blue, black and white livery to less fetching orange and white. At the same time the illuminated side panels were removed. Following BEA56's completion in 1969, the remainder of the fleet was completed between January and May 1970. *(Tony Wilson)*

double-deck bus built in the UK. It was 31ft 3in (9.53m) long and seated 72 passengers, but weighed only 8 tons 10 cwt (8.637 tonnes). Although work was commenced on four further prototypes, including one as a potential sales demonstrator, no further examples were completed after it was decided that London Transport's future lay in a fleet of single-deckers. The single completed vehicle had the potential for one-person operation and was converted to this mode in 1969.

One wonders how different the story of the London bus would have been if this single-deck Routemaster had been allowed to go into production? Between 1966 and 1979 London Transport bought some 1,500 single-deckers, followed by some 2,800 double-deckers, but these off-the-shelf vehicles were problematic and had a very short service life in the capital.

Maintenance and overhaul

When the Routemaster entered service the maintenance system operated by London Transport for its 12,000-strong bus fleet saw the overhaul of mechanical units carried out at Chiswick Works in West London and the overhaul of the bodywork carried out at Aldenham Works on the city's north-west outskirts. Day-to-day maintenance, including the replacement of mechanical units, was carried out at the local bus garages. The Routemaster had a reputation that an engine change could take place during the middle of the day – in hours rather than the days it took on more modern vehicles – and the bus could still be available for the morning and evening service!

With the reduction in fleet size and the cost-cutting culture of the 1980s, such luxuries as major overhaul depots could no longer be afforded, and Chiswick and Aldenham Works were closed in 1986 and 1990 respectively. In their day, both were famous for the quality of their workmanship. Chiswick could rebuild engines that would be deemed only suitable for scrap nowadays. It was also the home of the experimental department and the training school with the infamous skidpan.

Until June 1984 the Routemaster had

fitted into London Transport's programme at Aldenham Works, where the bodies and subframes were separated for overhaul. As is well documented elsewhere, this overhaul system completely mixed all the different batches of vehicles, so that, for example, Leyland-engined vehicles ended up spread throughout the fleet, and low-numbered bodies with non-opening upper-deck front windows could be found on practically any vehicle; however, exterior-advertisement bodies generally remained on the higher-numbered vehicles. Only the RMAs, RCLs and some RMLs didn't have any body changes.

Once the system of exchanging bodies during overhauls ceased the fleet became 'frozen' in this confused state, and remains so to this day.

The 1970s

In Routemaster terms, the 1970s are best remembered for a chronic shortage of spare parts. Much has been written about the inability of London Transport to cope with the mechanical specialities of modern rear-engined vehicles; a spare parts shortage that was primarily due to industrial action; and the late delivery of new vehicles. Combined, these factors resulted in vehicles having to be hired, and the purchase of non-standard and even second-hand vehicles. As noted below, the former BEA/British Airways RMAs were acquired together with the London Country and some Northern General vehicles, although none of the latter were prepared for normal service.

BELOW Early-numbered RM14 was 15 years old when this picture was taken in Walthamstow in May 1974. It carries the later-style livery of flake grey relief band, but with non-underlined gold fleet names. RM14 has carried non-opening upper-deck front windows throughout its life. (Tony Wilson)

Aldenham and the works float

ABOVE Aldenham Works was a special facility, and a place of mystery. The general public were rarely allowed inside its hallowed walls until it held open days towards the end of its existence. Here rows of bus bodies are lifted and moved around the cathedral-like works. *(London Transport Museum)*

RIGHT After initial examination, a Routemaster loses its public identity and its body is lifted from the front and rear subframes. The body and mechanical units are then overhauled separately, and upon completion of the overhaul the body was usually united with a different set of subframes and given a new public identity.
(London Transport Museum)

An important factor in the Routemaster being able to fit into the Aldenham Works overhaul system from the outset was the complete interchangeability of all its mechanical, electrical and bodywork components, whether large or small. The whole Routemaster fleet passed through the works between 1962 and 1986, with some vehicles being overhauled up to four times.

However, if you've ever tried to explain the game of cricket to aliens from another planet, you'll forgive me for labouring the next section...

Initially, a four-year cycle between overhauls was introduced for the Routemaster, but this was later increased to seven years, with an intermediate repaint. London Transport had a probably unique agreement with the Department of Transport, whereby until July 1982 the bodies and subframes were separated and overhauled separately before being reunited at the end of the process. However, it took far longer to overhaul the body and as a result the two parts that were reunited were rarely if ever the two that had entered the works together. For example, RM1234 would enter the works with body number B1234 and subframes A1234 (front) and B1234 (rear), but upon completion RM1234 could leave the works with body B1191 and subframes A1050 and B1050. Consequently during a vehicle's various overhaul cycles the bodies and subframes became thoroughly intermixed. The very last body to be lifted from its subframes at Aldenham was RM198 in June 1984 – all subsequent overhauls took place without the bodies and subframes being separated. However, many of the London Country RMLs and all of the RCL and RMA classes never underwent such changes of identity and retained matching elements throughout their lives.

As a consequence of this overhaul process, a 'works float' was established for each class of vehicle. This approximately equated to the number of vehicles in the works for overhaul at any one time, and any vehicle identity that became part of the works float was effectively in limbo for this period. Some vehicle identities

remained in the works float for many years. The explanation for this is that as a vehicle entered the works, it lost its fleet number and registration, and later on the same day this fleet number and registration would commonly reappear on another vehicle fresh from overhaul; in this way the road tax would never have to be surrendered and there would be a saving in the associated administration costs.

The actual identity of the vehicle was the body number together with its subframe unit numbers, and these identities remained with the units throughout their lives. It was common for the subframe units to remain together as a pair, the only exceptions being if a major repair was required or if the unit had to be replaced. It was only after Aldenham Works closed that these identities ceased to be used.

ABOVE In 1972 National Bus Company drab liveries became standard across their fleets; RCN694 succumbed to poppy red in August 1973, but by the time this photograph was taken two years later it had also lost its wheel trim and radiator grille trim. Despite its uncared-for look, the Northern General Routemasters had generally been reliable and were noted for their lack of corrosion when compared with other buses of the same age. It was ultimately the conversion to one-person-operation that caused these vehicles to be withdrawn. *(Tony Wilson)*

LEFT RM1999 was a regular on route 9 for 13 years, and became one of the Routemasters fitted with BESI (Bus Electronic Scanning Indicator) plates on the advert panels immediately above the front nearside wheel; this was an early system for the location of buses, to facilitate improved route regulation. Routemasters and route 9 appeared in a short 1976 British Transport Films feature entitled *The Nine Road. (Tony Wilson)*

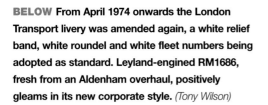

BELOW From April 1974 onwards the London Transport livery was amended again, a white relief band, white roundel and white fleet numbers being adopted as standard. Leyland-engined RM1686, fresh from an Aldenham overhaul, positively gleams in its new corporate style. *(Tony Wilson)*

BELOW Fifteen-year-old RM1149 awaits its next journey on route 117 alongside 24-year-old AEC Regal IV RF534. Although the latter survived another two years before being withdrawn and sold for preservation, the RM survived another nine years, then continued in passenger service for another eight years with two further operators before being finally withdrawn and exported to the Netherlands. *(Tony Wilson)*

ABOVE LEFT RMC1516 received three different all-over adverts between 1972 and 1975, the last of them being for the Fine Fare supermarket chain. By now it had been downgraded to bus work and was based at St Albans. It had lost its brake cooling grilles many years previously but had gained a radiator grille from an RCL or RML. *(Tony Wilson)*

ABOVE Within a year of the country operating area passing to the National Bus Company, a new logo appeared that was nicknamed the 'flying polo'. This was applied to the staircase panel on Routemasters. Although the cream-coloured relief band remains unchanged, the fleet name has been changed to 'London Country', now in yellow. *(Tony Wilson)*

Despite initial widely reported teething problems during the 1960s, after modifications the Routemaster became a very reliable workhorse, even during these difficult times. Some Routemasters that were awaiting repair or spare parts became heavily cannibalised in the mid-1970s, only to be rebuilt many years later and put back into service.

A notable date was 1 January 1970, when the former country area of London Transport was separated off and passed to the National Bus Company. With this transfer 69 RMCs, 43 RCLs and 97 RMLs passed to London Country Bus Services, a newly formed subsidiary of the National Bus Company.

Although RMs were replaced during the 1970s by modern one-person-operated types, the surplus RMs were used to replace RTs.

LEFT London Country RMC1519 appears to have a mixed identity, with cream and yellow relief band but yellow London Country fleet name and flying polo logo. It's another vehicle that had lost its brake-cooling grilles and gained a later-style radiator grille from an RCL or RML. *(Tony Wilson)*

ABOVE In the former central area the red RMLs were still earning their keep, and, with the failings of newer vehicles, they were about to enjoy a renaissance. The RML was now accepted as the most efficient vehicle in the fleet in terms of passengers carried and fuel consumption. RML2370 was 13 years old when this picture was taken and would soon be due for its second overhaul, but no one would have guessed that it still had 27 years of service life ahead of it. *(Tony Wilson)*

ABOVE Route 14 first gained an RM allocation in October 1963, and then RMLs from November 1966. With ever-increasing London traffic congestion the northern section, from Euston to Hornsey, was cut back in February 1987. One hundred RMLs were built with offside illuminated advert panels as displayed here on RML2660 carrying London Transport's own advertising. *(Tony Wilson)*

If things had gone as planned the modern types would have made inroads into the RM fleet in this way by the end of the decade. Approximately 60 RMs received light overhauls

BELOW Between June 1974 and October 1975, RM1255 carried this colourful all-over advert for the Rand employment agency. This was, of course, before the days of vinyl, and these adverts were painted *by hand*. When RM1255 was completed in June 1962 it was the first production RM to be fitted with a Leyland engine. *(Tony Wilson)*

in 1972 to keep them operational for just three years, but from the middle of the decade new deliveries were used to replace unsuitable one-person-operated single-deck classes, and this delayed the plan to replace the Routemasters. Consequently the 60 RMs overhauled in 1972 were later overhauled again, and remained in service with the rest of the fleet.

The years between 1969 and 1975 were the peak period of 'all-over advert' buses in London, including 20 RMs and seven RMLs so painted, of which some received such advertising liveries twice. The very first Routemaster decorated in this fashion was RM1737, advertising Silexine Paints, which is now exhibited in the London Transport Museum in Covent Garden, albeit back in standard red livery.

Other later special liveries included 25 RMs painted silver for the silver jubilee of HM Queen Elizabeth II in 1977, 12 RMs painted in 'Shillibeer' livery in 1979, 16 RMs painted in red and yellow 'Shoplinker' livery, also in 1979, six RMs painted as large parcels for the Royal Wedding in 1981, and six special liveries, including gold-painted RM1983 in 1983 for the 50th anniversary of London Transport.

ABOVE The Silver Jubilee of HM Queen Elizabeth II in 1977 was commemorated by a fleet of 25 Routemasters suitably repainted silver. They ran between April and November of that year and were numbered in their own SRM series. They were each sponsored by various companies, with SRM4 (RM1889) being sponsored by the Amey Roadstone Corporation. *(Tony Wilson)*

ABOVE RIGHT All 25 SRMs were fitted with 100% wool carpets on the gangways of both decks, supplied by the International Wool Secretariat. After completion of the Jubilee contract one of the carpets was cleaned to show how well they'd survived everyday London service. This particular RM has Permatread flooring under the seats; this hard-wearing material was fitted by Aldenham Works in the 1970s, and later to RMLs as part of the 1990s refurbishment programme. *(London Transport)*

RIGHT For the 150th anniversary of George Shillibeer's original London Omnibus in 1979, 12 RMs were repainted at Aldenham works in this superb livery. As with the SRMs sponsors were sought, and the buses ran from March 1979 to early 1980. Former London Country RCL2221 was also outshopped in this livery, but was used as an exhibition and cinema bus for London Transport. *(Tony Wilson)*

BELOW For the wedding of HRH Prince Charles and Lady Diana Spencer in July 1981, six RMs were outshopped in a special 'parcel bus' livery in June that even featured a large bow on the roof for people looking down from overhead. Once again sponsors were sought. All eight vehicles returned to normal fleet livery by October of that year. *(Tony Wilson)*

BELOW In 1983 various special liveries were carried by London's buses to commemorate 50 years of London Transport's existence. Appropriately, RM1983 was repainted gold in April of that year and remained in this livery until repainted red in February 1984. Four other RMs were repainted by individual garages in a replica of 1933 London bus livery. *(Andrew Morgan)*

ABOVE By April 1977 RMC1496 had less than two years' service left with London Country. It's seen here in full National Bus Company livery in West Croydon, but was later repainted red for use as a training bus with London Transport. Following a refurbishment in 1989 it formed part of the dedicated fleet for the new Beckton Express X15 from the City of London to the rejuvenating Docklands. After being declared surplus it completed two tours with the Cliff Richard Tennis Trail before being sold in 1994, and has since worked for several companies as a promotional bus. *(Tony Wilson)*

BELOW Another livery change occurred after the merger of BOAC and BEA to form British Airways in 1973, 52 of their fleet having gained the new company's navy blue and white livery by early 1975. A unique feature of this fleet's operations was its service along the M4 Motorway; with their larger engines and rear axles they were often quoted as being capable of running at over 60mph (96kph). *(Tony Wilson)*

The beginning of the end and life after London

The first withdrawals of Routemasters from service were commenced by British Airways (formerly BEA) in 1975, followed by Northern General and London Country in the late 1970s and by London Transport from 1982 onwards. In total nearly 1,600 Routemasters have been scrapped, but many have been sold for further service around the United Kingdom or around the world; others have been used for a variety of non-passenger-carrying duties and numerous examples have been preserved by enthusiasts.

The first of the BEA Routemasters was withdrawn in 1975, and following further reductions in the airport service all their remaining vehicles were acquired by London Transport between 1975 and 1979 and numbered in a new sequence as the RMA class. After initial trials with the first 13 in passenger service in 1975, many were employed as staff buses to and from Aldenham and Chiswick Works, with seven converted as training buses in 1981. However, London Transport never used all of them, and sales of surplus vehicles commenced in 1981. Initially some went for scrap, but from 1982 onwards some were sold for preservation.

At the end of 1986 six RMAs had been repainted and fitted with front blind boxes before transfer from Bus Engineering Limited (BEL) at Chiswick Works to the then new Tours and Charter fleet for sightseeing work in London.

The remaining RMAs left with London Transport's successor, London Buses, continued in use as trainers and were only sold off as they became surplus. Operating subsidiary East London refurbished two RMAs in 1989 and 1991 respectively, initially for use on route X15 Beckton Express and later alongside standard vehicles on route 15 until converted to open-top and exported to Portugal in 1998.

Once London Country became part of the National Bus Company the crew-operated vehicles were a threatened species. Early in the 1970s the RMCs and RCLs were relegated from Green Line services to ordinary bus work, replacing RTs. Hence it was only a matter of time before they would be replaced by one-person-operated vehicles.

Between 1977 and 1980 the surplus London Country vehicles were withdrawn and stored, only to be later reacquired by London Transport. The RMCs and RCLs were initially used as trainers, but the RMLs were overhauled and returned to service at a time when Routemasters were very sought-after. In fact all but 19 of the 97 RMLs were returned to service and became intermixed with the original red examples, the remainder being scrapped.

Altogether 66 of the production batch of 68 RMCs were reacquired and retained by London Transport. Up to the time of the privatisation of London Buses' operating companies these were progressively withdrawn and sold, either after accidents or simply as surplus. Three RMCs were saved from scrap and converted to open-top types for special duties, while in 1989 East London renovated seven examples for use on the new route X15 Beckton Express. This route was converted to one-person operation in 1991, when these vehicles were found other duties.

Similarly, 41 of the 43 RCLs were reacquired and retained by London Transport, and after some of them were used as trainers 40 were overhauled at Aldenham Works. They re-entered passenger service from August 1980 at Edmonton and Stamford Hill garages, but with single headlamps fitted and the platform doors removed. Internally, the luggage racks had been taken out, a bell cord fitted in the lower saloon and the seats retrimmed in 1970s standard blue moquette. Although externally they had a passing resemblance to the RMLs, internally they kept their lower seating capacity.

ABOVE LEFT RML2414 is at the end of its days with London Country, but displays several oddities including an RM nearside wing and a kerb-guide. The kerb-guide was fitted to some of the London Country RML fleet to assist drivers in keeping the front of the vehicle on the road and away from the kerb. *(Tony Wilson)*

ABOVE RCL2249 was one the final three RCLs that remained in service. It's seen here less than a year before it was withdrawn from operation with London Country and is in typical condition, with severely dented roof dome. Upon sale to London Transport in February 1979 it saw immediate use as a trainer. *(Tony Wilson)*

The remaining vehicle was RCL2221, which was converted to a mobile cinema and exhibition bus for the 1979 Shillibeer celebrations. After many years of spasmodic use it was sold to Timebus Travel in 2008 and continues in use as an exhibition vehicle that's available for hire.

After only three years' service the RCLs were deemed below standard and were all withdrawn by the end of 1984, being replaced by the then surplus standard RMs. In early 1986 the remaining 11 vehicles in stock were sent to Aldenham Works for overhaul as part of London Buses' new Tours and Charter fleet (later renamed London Coaches) for sightseeing work.

The 51 Routemasters at Northern General were similarly withdrawn to make way for one-person operation. Although they had lasted up to 15 years in service (from 1964 to 1980), it's widely agreed that they could probably have kept going for much longer, as they were actually in better condition than rear-engined

vehicles of similar age. The first batch of
Northern General vehicles was sold off in 1977,
most of them going direct to dealers. However,
in 1978 London Transport acquired two that
were subsequently stripped for spares at the
Wombwell Diesels scrapyard. In 1979–80 12
more were acquired with the much mooted
idea of overhauling them at Aldenham Works
and returning them to service, but this time in
London; they were subsequently resold in 1981
after seeing no service with London Transport.

One of the dealers who bought RMFs at this
time was Brakell Omnibus Sales, who repainted
some of them red and leased them to London
Transport for sightseeing work. They were even
numbered in a series from RMF2761, although
when London Transport themselves started to
acquire the type they were hastily renumbered
from RMF2791. Several preservationists
purchased some at this time, as they were
the only Routemasters available to private
individuals. Unfortunately not many have
survived and only 14 are known to exist today,
nine of them in the British Isles.

Sales of the first standard London
Routemasters commenced in September 1972,
when RML2691 was sold to Gala Cosmetics
for use as a mobile beauty salon with Mary
Quant. Five RMs were scrapped in 1974 after
fire or major collision damage. Only two other
central area RMLs have been sold, these being
900 and 2557. The latter was fire-damaged in
1983, while the former was an accident victim
and was deemed by London Buses to be
uneconomical to repair; in February 1988 the
then Clydeside Scottish bought it and rebuilt
it at their Johnstone workshops using parts
from RM1984. By the end of June 1988 it had
re-entered service, but this time north of the
border in the Glasgow area. Early in 1995 it
was purchased by Blue Triangle at Rainham, for
whom it entered service in December 2003 and
with whom it remains.

The first quantity disposals from London
were dictated by politics. The Labour Party
took control of Greater London Council in the
elections of May 1981 and swiftly moved to
implement their 'Fares Fair' programme. Fares

were cut by an average of 32% on all London Transport buses and the Underground services from October 1981, and the passengers they daily carried rose from five-and-a-half to six million. The increased subsidy required by London Transport was partly funded from the rates, which in turn had to be increased. This met with opposition from ratepayers, and the London Borough of Bromley contested the legality of the subsidies in the Courts, with the result that the Law Lords declared them to be unlawful. Consequently on 21 March 1982 London Transport fares were increased, in effect doubling overnight and thus becoming 33% higher than before the introduction of the Fares Fair policy. Inevitably, passenger journeys dropped back to five million per day, which led to large-scale cuts and service revisions on 4 September, including the initiation of London Routemaster withdrawals. Overnight the capital's scheduled vehicle requirement was reduced by 244 Routemasters.

By the end of the year 61 RMs had been sold and a further 98 were wholly or partly broken up at Aldenham Works. The first of these sales took place in October, with 51 passing to W. North's of Sherburn-in-Elmet for scrap, with the parts being returned to London Buses; seven more were written off for scrap, and four RMs were exported to Japan. These had actually left the country in August, initially for display at the Matsuda collection.

After these unhappy months, withdrawals of Routemasters continued until late 1988 due to the steady conversion of routes to one-

person operation. The RML fleet continued to remain intact, with RMs being replaced by any surplus RMLs. The first withdrawals were of vehicles fitted with what was deemed to be non-standard equipment, eg Leyland engines and Simms electrical components. In 1985 the emphasis changed to vehicles that were due for their fifth body overhaul.

In late 1984 RMs 1288 and 1873 were exported to Hong Kong in the hope that China might become a large export market. RM1288 was rebuilt at Aldenham Works with a nearside staircase and offside platform. Unfortunately the much-rumoured sale of up to 1,300 buses to China never materialised, and RM1288 and another two vehicles exported to Hong Kong in 1991 remain the only Routemasters sent to this part of the Far East.

The following year, Stagecoach – the then small independent Scottish-based operator from the Perth area – purchased five Leyland-engined Routemasters, which were the first of the type to operate north of the border. Later that year Clydeside Scottish Omnibuses Ltd were lent RM652 for an open day and retained it for trials around the Glasgow outskirts. (Clydeside was one of the new subsidiaries of the Scottish Bus Group, formed in 1985 in preparation for bus deregulation scheduled for 26 October 1986.) After the success of these trials, Clydeside went on to acquire and operate over 70 Routemasters. Another recently-formed company, Kelvin Scottish, borrowed several Routemasters from Clydeside and then established a fleet of over 50 vehicles

ABOVE LEFT Some 30 Routemasters in standard London service have been painted in all-over adverts at some time, with most of these appearing in the early 1970s until public opinion turned against them. Three that appeared in the mid-1980s included RML2492 in this garish yellow and green livery from June 1984 to August 1985 on behalf of Underwoods. *(Andrew Morgan)*

ABOVE RML2718 is in typical mid-1980s condition, including 'L'-shaped advert and advert frames. The advert frames were a new idea adopted to stop damage to bodywork and to make advert-changing quicker and easier. The adverts were now applied directly to pre-cut boards that slid into the frames along the sides of the vehicle. *(Andrew Morgan)*

ABOVE Kelvin Scottish operated up to 68 Routemasters in the north Glasgow area from 1986 to 1993. All came from London Buses, but RM858 only lasted four years before being sold for scrap in 1990. Two years after being acquired it lost its London plates and was assigned an anonymous Scottish registration, EDS362A. One wonders if its original WLT858 plates are still on a private car today. *(Andrew Morgan)*

ABOVE One of the most striking liveries was that worn by the first batch of Routemasters acquired by Strathtay Scottish for operation in Perth and Dundee. In late October sunshine, RM1911 is seen here in Perth in 1986. It remained with Strathtay until 1992 and was then exported to Hungary. *(Andrew Morgan)*

of its own. In this way the Scottish Bus Group was able to compete directly with its long-time rival Strathclyde PTE. Another new Scottish Bus Group company, Strathtay Scottish, also conducted successful trials and acquired over 20 vehicles for use in Perth and Dundee.

The Routemaster was suddenly seen as the ideal tool in the competitive battle for passengers around the United Kingdom. Their relatively fast operation, combined with a friendly crew and their reasonable initial costs for a well-maintained vehicle, were all advantages that appealed instantly to operators up and down the country.

RIGHT From 1986 until 1996 Blackpool Transport operated a fleet of Routemasters on various routes, including along the famous promenade. All but one of these vehicles were Leyland-engined and many, including RM1640, went on to see further service with Reading Mainline. RM1640 returned to London service in 2001 and continues to operate on heritage route 9. *(Andrew Morgan)*

In this way a new chapter of the Routemaster story commenced in 1985, when examples were acquired by operators around the British Isles for use in the newly privatised and deregulated motorbus world. (Bus services in London remained regulated and, unlike the rest of the UK, deregulation did not occur in October 1986.) By the late 1980s examples could be seen operating in Southampton, Blackpool, Glasgow, Perth, Dundee, Hull, Carlisle, Bedford, Kettering, Manchester, Southend and Burnley, to name just some of the major operations. At the time, George Watson, general manager of Clydeside Scottish, was quoted as saying: 'The RMs benefited from regular and excellent maintenance at Aldenham and Chiswick Works in London. This meant that when we bought what was on paper a 20/25 year old vehicle, in practice it was the condition of a vehicle that was perhaps only five years old.' Sadly, however, during the early 1990s – with a recession biting hard – rationalisation became the name of the game, and most surviving Routemaster operations were withdrawn.

1990s developments

One of the most interesting of these involved the London sightseeing scene. By the mid-1980s successful sightseeing tours had been set up by various operators, many of which involved the use of former London buses. However, London Transport's own share of this market had reduced as more operators entered the market.

ABOVE LEFT Like Blackpool Transport, Southampton City Transport favoured the Leyland-engined variety of Routemaster and acquired them to defend its routes against competition from then-new operator Solent Blue Line. RM2005 operated in Southampton for a year and then passed to Southend Transport before finding a new home near Dublin with Dualway Coaches. Tragically this vehicle was destroyed in an arson attack in early 2011. *(Andrew Morgan)*

ABOVE The BEA/British Airways front-entrance Routemasters have always been a rarity to find in normal passenger service. Here, BEA34 – or RMA50, as it became renumbered when acquired by London Transport in 1979 – is operating a school duty in 1992 for Kelvin Central, from Cambuslang school, but still retains the livery of its former owner, Stagecoach. The following year it went back to Stagecoach before passing to Lothian Buses in Edinburgh, and then in 2009 to Essex-based operator Ensign Bus. *(Andrew Morgan)*

Consequently it was relaunched for the 1986 season with 50 Routemasters and re-marketed as 'the Original London Transport Sightseeing Tour'. All of the vehicles were prepared at Aldenham Works and converted for their new role. The remaining 11 RCLs left in stock were allocated to the fleet together with 39 RMs. Twenty of the RMs were converted to open-top. Prior to the commencement of the new season Aldenham Works overhauled the entire fleet and repainted them in 1960s livery with a cream band and underlined gold fleet names.

Changes to the fleet quickly saw two of the RMs converted to open-top, and in the autumn the RCLs were fitted with modern platform doors. At the end of 1986 six surplus former RMA staff buses were acquired from Bus Engineering and were repainted and

ABOVE London Coaches RM163 is fully loaded with paying tourists as it approaches Horse Guards Parade. It was rebuilt to open-top layout in the summer of 1986 and was later rebuilt for the 1990 season, but this time as the first of the ten longer ERM vehicles. It remained in service in London until 2001, before being sold for further sightseeing service the following year in Edinburgh.
(Andrew Morgan)

retrimmed at Aldenham Works prior to joining the sightseeing fleet. Two additional open-top RMs were acquired in 1987 in exchange for three closed-top RMs that were declared surplus; these had previously been used at the Liverpool Garden Festival in 1986. For the 1988 season a further seven RMs were converted to open-top, but this time by outside contractors, as Aldenham Works had by now been closed. Two of these were unique in being fitted with a nearside wheelchair lift. A further oddity was RM545, which became the first RM to be re-engined with a non-standard unit when it was fitted with an 11.6-litre DAF DK 1160VS in 1988.

Although the sightseeing operation was very successful, the most popular attraction in the summer months was the upper deck, especially in good weather; however, compared with more modern double-deckers the relatively short Routemaster had a low upper-deck seating capacity of just 36. An idea was consequently mooted of lengthening the Routemaster body by inserting an extra bay into the middle. Therefore in early 1990 open-top RM163 had its body dismantled and a complete bay inserted. The resulting conversion was a 32ft 6in (9.91m) vehicle with a 21ft 6in (6.56m) wheelbase and upper-deck seating capacity of 44; this was

the longest type of Routemaster ever built (or in this case rebuilt). Nine further buses were similarly converted, the ten donor vehicles being obtained from surplus Routemasters stored ready for sale. A by-product of this conversion programme was that the donor vehicles were then bolted back together – to create the shortest RM variant at only 23ft (7.01m) – so that they could be taken away for scrap.

Further conversions within this fleet were less major, but still took advantage of the Routemaster's jig-built construction. For instance, in April 1990 two RMs – followed in October 1991 by two more – were fitted with the rear ends and platform doors from withdrawn RMCs. Also in 1990 two RCLs were converted to open-top types and reseated to achieve increased upper-deck capacity.

To resolve the continuing issue of having vehicles that could be used only in good summer weather, not in inclement weather (and vice versa), the next conversions, in mid-1991, saw ten RCLs and four RMs rebuilt with a convertible open-top roof. As these conversions were completed, six open-top RMs were sold as surplus.

During this time various liveries and all-over adverts were carried by some of this fleet, as the requirement to remain in London red livery was no longer deemed to be important.

On 18 May 1992 this fleet became the first London Buses subsidiary to be privatised, as London Coaches. Included within the sale were 46 Routemasters.

Further fleet reductions occurred in 1993–94, with three open-top RMs and then the six RMAs being sold, followed by three RMs and one RCL in 1997. On 4 December 1997 the remainder of the fleet was acquired by Arriva, and in 1998 vehicles appeared in a revised Arriva-style livery. Further RM withdrawals quickly occurred and 2001 was their last season on sightseeing duties in London.

Big Bus was another competitor in the London sightseeing market and between 1992 and 2003 they operated one RM and three RMFs on their tours. All remained closed-top, but their first RMF was acquired in open-top format.

After 1990 the pace of withdrawals in London slowed and stopped, as there was no obvious

replacement for the fleet in central London. As the privatisation of the operating companies approached the fleet remained intact, and the core fleet of Routemasters survived.

Between 1990 and 1994 all but two of the surviving 502-strong RML fleet, together with more than a hundred RMs, were re-engined with new Cummins or Iveco units. In addition, between 1992 and 1994 the 500 RMLs were refurbished for a widely quoted 'further ten years' service.

At the end of 1994 the privatisation of the London Buses operating subsidiaries was completed and most of the Routemasters in the capital were thereafter in private ownership. However, the 43 RMLs then in use on routes 13 and 19 remained owned by London Transport, and although some of these subsequently moved to other routes they were still leased to the operators by London Regional Transport and its successor Transport *for* London (formed in 2000) until the end of mainstream

BELOW The RML refurbishment programme completed between 1992 and 1994 was carried out by three contractors: TBP Holdings Limited of Birmingham, South Yorkshire Transport at Rotherham and Leaside Buses of Enfield. In March 1993 freshly completed RML2657 operates a special working on route 25 before this route was shortened.
(Andrew Morgan)

Routemaster operations. At this time just over 500 Routemasters were required for service on a daily basis in London, and a fleet of around 620 was owned or leased to service this requirement.

A further variation to the standard Routemaster specification occurred in 1996 when Scania engines were fitted to London Central's RM fleet for route 36, followed by the majority of the Stagecoach Routemaster fleet and several of the Arriva London RMs.

All but one of the London Routemaster routes were re-tendered between September 1996 and July 2000. All of them continued to be operated by Routemaster vehicles for a further period except route 139, which was operated by London Northern and was converted to low-floor Dennis Dart operation in March 1998. All surplus RMs from this route were quickly sold and again went mostly to dealers for resale, predominantly to buyers abroad. With each tender announcement it became noteworthy that the number of crew vehicles required often actually increased, as the proposed frequency required by London Transport Buses likewise increased. Hence during the post-privatisation period the number of surplus Routemasters available for service diminished and accident-damaged vehicles were usually repaired, often at any cost. The number of vehicles actually scrapped in this period was very low indeed.

The surplus vehicles that were not retained in their Reserve Fleet by London Buses at the end of 1994, following the privatisation of the operating companies, were sold to dealer PVS

at Barnsley, and these have very slowly been scrapped, with any salvageable parts being recovered from them. Some have been saved for restoration after standing stripped in this scrapyard for 17 years (see Chapter 3).

Reading Mainline was the last sizeable Routemaster operator outside London, which commenced operations on 23 July 1994. In total 43 vehicles were acquired, including many from operators around the British Isles as well as a few former preserved examples. The last vehicles to be purchased were the complete batch of 12 Leyland-engined RMs from Blackpool Transport in early 1997, which had last seen service in September 1996. Reading Mainline was sold to Reading Buses on 2 June 1998, a condition of the transaction being that it should continue operating for a further two years; in actual fact it ran for two years and one month. The final day of operation was 22 July 2000, when only two routes (lines D and F) were still operating and a total of 11 RMs were available for service.

Renaissance and the end in London

In an amazing turnaround, in 2000 London Buses bought back 50 Routemasters that hade been previously sold off as redundant. Transport *for* London had been newly formed, and with Ken Livingstone as the new Mayor of London the Routemaster was back in favour. Livingstone made several pledges with regard to the future of Routemaster operation, and in particular crew operation of buses in London. (He also made pledges with regard to the long-term replacement of the Routemaster fleet, but this, of course, never happened. There was also the famous statement made by him in 2001 that 'Only some ghastly dehumanised moron would want to get rid of the Routemaster', so its future all looked very positive in 2000–1.)

After a major refurbishment, 49 of the 50 reacquired Routemasters re-entered passenger service on the streets of London, and with the latest technology of Cummins Euro II engines they were at the time among the greenest buses in the city. A spin-off from this programme saw nearly 50 further vehicles provided with the same engines but not cosmetically refurbished. The Cummins Euro II had become familiar in the Dennis Dart single-decker, and the converted Routemasters were consequently quickly nicknamed 'Dartmasters'.

The 2002 Golden Jubilee of HM Queen Elizabeth II saw 15 Routemasters (three RMs and twelve RMLs) given an overall gold livery. Surprisingly, none of these featured in the launch publicity, and maybe this was the beginning of the end as the tide turned against the Routemaster in London. RM6 retains its gold livery to this day, and is now part of the Arriva London Heritage fleet.

Meanwhile in Edinburgh, the Mac Tours sightseeing operation converted to Routemasters in 2002, with vehicles sourced from all over the British Isles. A fleet of more than 20 open-top, convertible open-top, closed-top and part open-top vehicles was acquired, made up of RM, RMC, RCL and all

ten of the longer ERM vehicles. The whole fleet was refurbished for its new role. New platform doors were fitted and in 2003–4 a programme was undertaken to fit the same environmentally friendly Cummins engines as were used in London. In early 2009 surplus vehicles from this fleet were sold off and it has stabilised at ten ERMs, two RCLs and one RM. Several have now been further rebuilt so that the fleet has a mixed collection of five part open-top and the rest (all ERMs) fully open-top.

BELOW The Golden Jubilee of HM Queen Elizabeth II in 2002 was commemorated by a fleet of 50 London buses suitably reliveried in gold, including 15 Routemasters. The Routemasters ran in service between March that year and the following February. They were each sponsored by one of five companies, with RML2414 being sponsored by Nestlé's (Felix cat food). This photograph shows up the panels that were vinyled and the lighter ones that were painted. *(Geoff Rixon)*

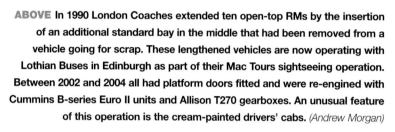

ABOVE In 1990 London Coaches extended ten open-top RMs by the insertion of an additional standard bay in the middle that had been removed from a vehicle going for scrap. These lengthened vehicles are now operating with Lothian Buses in Edinburgh as part of their Mac Tours sightseeing operation. Between 2002 and 2004 all had platform doors fitted and were re-engined with Cummins B-series Euro II units and Allison T270 gearboxes. An unusual feature of this operation is the cream-painted drivers' cabs. *(Andrew Morgan)*

ABOVE All Routemasters with Lothian Buses have been retrimmed in tartan, with vinyl on the exposed upper deck and moquette on the lower deck. The areas that were previously burgundy are now cream with red edging. New flooring has also been laid in preparation for entering service with Lothian. *(Andrew Morgan)*

As detailed above, from 1996 onwards London Transport Buses offered individual contracts for the 20 Routemaster-operated routes in central London. Up until the summer of 2003 all but one of these routes remained with Routemasters. However, from this time on, one by one, all Routemaster-operated routes were gradually converted to the latest type of vehicles, namely low-floor double-deckers and, for two routes, articulated 'bendy' buses.

For the record, at the beginning of February 2003 a maximum of 574 Routemasters was required to service 20 central London routes. To achieve this, the various London operating companies owned or leased a total of 643 RMs and RMLs; however, to be 100% accurate, this maximum number was never actually achieved, as several routes required more vehicles to increase the frequency of service, particularly at the end of 2002, which therefore increased

RIGHT The retrimmed lower deck also shows the original sliding bulkhead window behind the driver's cab and the pair of seats that are positioned longitudinally. *(Andrew Morgan)*

daily peak vehicle requirement. At this time the London Routemaster fleet was fully stretched and many doored buses were seen alongside the Routemasters on several routes on a daily basis in order to achieve the required number of vehicles.

From the summer of 2003 volume sales of Routemasters recommenced as Transport *for* London resumed its plan to replace conductors with new-style ticketing and boarding systems. Indeed, one of the saddest changes resulting from the scrapping of the Routemaster was that conductors on London buses would also be consigned to the history books. The reason behind this policy was often quoted as being the fact that less than 10% of fares were now paid on board the bus, with the remainder being taken before starting a journey. By 2002 there was also considerable pressure from the powerful disability lobby for fully accessible vehicles. The resulting surplus vehicles were quickly sold on to new owners across the British Isles and around the world.

Not forgetting the partial conversions of routes 10 and 36 in February 2003, the first of the final tranche of route conversions took place on 30 August 2003 when route 15 lost its Routemasters. As the conversions progressed, each change was marked in various special ways, usually by the operation of special 'guest' vehicles on the service's last day (or days). Many of these 'guest' vehicles were from other companies and included the earlier RT type in recognition of the route's history and the passing of the conductor. Sadly, during this period no major work was carried out on the main fleet except for standard maintenance, with the result that most of the fleet looked very down at heel as it was withdrawn. The final much-delayed three refurbishments were completed on behalf of Transport *for* London in March 2004, with the re-engining programme completed only in 2002. Unusually, during this period accident-damaged vehicles were sold rather than repaired, to quickly reappear with new owners after being fixed.

Another unusual aspect of this final withdrawal programme was that the vehicles were all resold to new owners, often via dealers, and many have since been used for further passenger service. Only a small handful of

the 600 Routemasters withdrawn and sold have been scrapped. (See Appendix B for a summary of surviving Routemasters.)

September 2004 marked the 50th anniversary of RM1's debut, and a suitable commemorative event was held in London with nearly a hundred vehicles in attendance. Numerous buses operated by Arriva and Go Ahead London carried large, round, white and gold 'Routemaster 50' logos during the summer to mark the anniversary.

A major route conversion on 3 September 2004 resulted in 94 less Routemasters being required, with three routes losing all their Routemasters on the same day. One of these was route 73, with its massive requirement of 55 vehicles. Supporting the Cummins-engined RMLs on this service was AEC-engined RM5. This route had seen 42 years' continuous operation by Routemasters, and although not the longest period of service the demise of this well-known route nevertheless marked the passing of a landmark. RM5 duly operated the very last journey, and went into the history books as the last AEC-engined bus in regular service in London. It was subsequently retained for use by Arriva London's Heritage fleet until 2008 and has since been privately acquired and extensively restored, although it is still maintained and garaged by Arriva London.

At the beginning of 2005 just seven Routemaster-operated routes remained in

BELOW A contrast of London operators: the Stagecoach London route 15 RML on the right has a matter of months to go before withdrawal, but the London Central route 36 RML has been repainted, re-engined with a Cummins B-series Euro II and an Allison T270 gearbox, and had hopper windows fitted. This re-engined vehicle was one of those that had been withdrawn by London Country that then completed a further 25 years of service on busy routes in central London. However, it was only a matter of time before route 36 would also lose its Routemasters, and its time was up in January 2005.

(Mark Kehoe)

ABOVE April 2005, and Piccadilly is still full of Routemasters. One by one their services were converted, in April (route 19), July (routes 14 and 22) and finally October (route 38). Arriva London's RML2359 leads four RMLs alongside another London icon, the FX4 taxi.

(Mark Kehoe)

London, for which 192 vehicles were required. The Mayor for London had meanwhile announced that 100% of the London bus network would be operated by low-floor buses by the end of the year, and as months went by it became known that the final mainstream Routemaster-operated service would be route 159. This busy service operated from Marble Arch to Streatham station and had a peak vehicle requirement (PVR) of 31 Routemasters. When route 137 had been converted in July 2004 the longer but less presentable RMLs were retained for use on route 159. However, many of these were failing by this time and the refurbished Transport *for* London-owned RMs were substituted, and by its final days the route was operated by a mixture of Iveco-engined RMLs and Cummins-engined RMs.

Friday 9 December was set as the date for the conversion. However, an unusual decision was made that the final vehicle would operate at lunchtime, with vehicles being progressively changed over during the daylight hours. Therefore a final day special operation was set for the Thursday, which saw 24 guest vehicles operating on the route alongside its regular 31 vehicles, although some only saw brief service or made just a few journeys. Among the notable Routemaster vehicles used were the very first and the very last, RM1 and RML2760. By now it had become customary for there to be large media coverage of such events, including numerous television crews. There had never been the passing of a bus like it.

And so the last official Routemaster journey

on route 159 left Marble Arch at 12:52, operated by RM2217 – numerically the last RM, which had recently been refurbished by Arriva London for their Heritage fleet and had been held back from standard service for the final day. It was preceded by other Routemasters from the Arriva Heritage fleet, namely RM5 and gold-liveried RM6. RM2217 arrived at its terminus at Streatham Hill (which is actually Brixton bus garage) at 14:03. However, one of the service RMs, RM54, which was ahead of the trio of final vehicles, was actually running over an hour late, and arrived at the Streatham Station terminus at 14:09, thereby becoming the last mainstream Routemaster-operated service carrying fare-paying passengers. For the record, the last RML in passenger service on route 159 was RML2491.

Every junction and vantage point along the route, as well as at Brixton itself, was overflowing with people. These were not just enthusiasts, but ordinary members of the public waving farewell to a lifelong friend and witnessing a notable date in transport history that marked the passing of both the bus conductor and the Routemaster from mainstream London service.

However, alongside all this doom and gloom as the Routemaster reached the end of its time in regular London service – despite the Mayor's earlier declaration that Routemasters would remain on the city's streets – in May 2005 it was announced that two Heritage routes were to operate in central London, and it became clear that they would be running in parallel to parts of two existing routes. After a tendering exercise, on 9 September it was announced that these would be awarded to First London and Stagecoach East London, and would operate over part of route 9 and part of route 15. The services were launched on 14 November, utilising ten of the Transport *for* London-owned refurbished vehicles that had recently been freed up from other routes, and initially running from 09:30 to 18:30, seven days a week, at 15-minute intervals.

The London Heritage routes see occasional running days on Sundays, when, in the spirit of the last days of various Routemaster-operated routes in London, various guest vehicles are allowed to run as duplicates or in place of the standard allocation.

In late 2009 the two Heritage routes were re-tendered by Transport *for* London and in May 2010 it was announced that they had been retained by their present operators. The new five-year contracts commenced from 13 November 2010. At the same time the course of route 9 was amended and the frequency of service was reduced from 15 to 20 minutes.

So in the end the Mayor of London was correct: you *can* still ride on Routemasters in London, although only on short routes operating alongside existing low-floor double-deckers. In theory these routes fully comply with DDA legislation due to come into force in 2017, so hopefully some form of Routemaster operation will continue in the capital for many years to come.

But what happened to the 600 vehicles that were withdrawn? As noted above, all but a very small handful survive and generally they have all found new homes and new uses. Many have been exported from the UK but many others have been acquired by operating companies and are available for private hire or occasional passenger service across the country. (See Chapter 5 for more details of where to find and ride on Routemasters.)

The Routemaster may well be the last bus designed and built specially for London; even though, in the 21st century, Transport *for* London has launched its own 'New bus for London' project the line of true descent has been severed, and probably no new bus will

ABOVE **An RM refurbishment programme commenced in 2000, with 43 being completed by Marshall Bus, followed by a further six by Arriva London. This enabled a more modern and environmentally friendly mechanical specification to be achieved. The merits of the hopper windows could be questioned, but apart from cosmetic enhancements the bodywork remained mostly intact. RM1280 was the first RM to be re-engined with the Cummins B-series Euro II and Allison MT643 gearbox, and ended up being allocated to route 159 right up until its conversion on 9 December 2005.** *(Mark Kehoe)*

ever win the hearts and minds of Londoners in the same way as the Routemaster and the numerous types that preceded it.

Meanwhile, after nearly 60 years, and with over 40% of all Routemasters built still surviving, the story of this legend continues.

LEFT **This was the scene as Arriva London's RM2217 returned to Brixton garage on route 159 on 9 December 2005, to become the last official Routemaster in mainstream passenger service. Not only was this the end of the Routemaster on a main route, but it was also the end of the bus conductor.**
(Mark Kehoe)

Chapter Two

Anatomy of the Routemaster

The Routemaster is an integrally constructed double-decker with steel subframes and aluminium jig-built bodywork, with an automatic gearbox, power steering, independent suspension, power hydraulic brakes and passenger compartment heating all as standard; for a 1950s design these were advanced features. It was built to fit into London Transport's standard maintenance procedures and was completed to a high standard of finish in order to attract the type of passenger that was then buying cars.

OPPOSITE This view of an AEC AV590 being lifted back into the engine bay of RM5 during its restoration shows the easy access to the front of the vehicle. Routemasters were designed to be easy to maintain, as well as for the quick and efficient changing of units. *(Phil Swallow)*

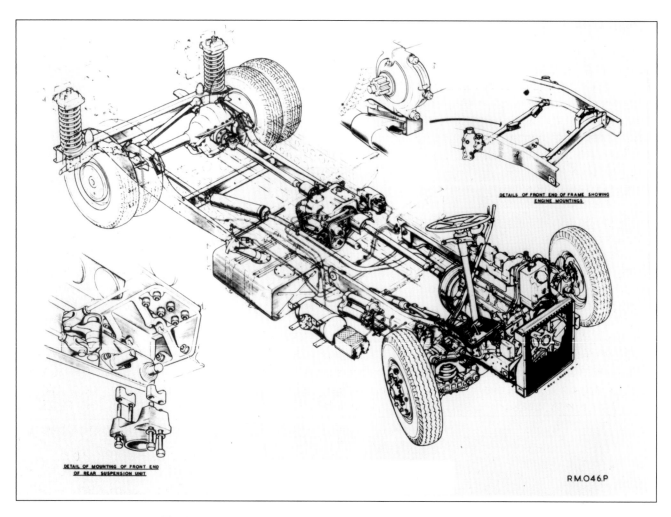

DETAILS OF FRONT END OF FRAME SHOWING ENGINE MOUNTINGS

DETAIL OF MOUNTING OF FRONT END OF REAR SUSPENSION UNIT

R.M.046.P

The following description is based on Maintenance Bulletin No 47 issued by London Transport in 1961, and covers the standard AEC-engined Routemaster that was for so long the most common type in service.

Subframes

The main mechanical units are carried by a pair of subframes in place of the customary one-piece chassis assembly. The front subframe is known as the A-frame and carries the engine, steering column, pedal gear and front axle. The rear subframe is known as the B-frame and carries the rear axle and suspension assemblies.

The A-frame consists of a pair of steel channel members which are cantilevered forward of the front bulkhead of the body structure and extend rearwards to the second main crossmember of the floor. It is attached to the front bulkhead by two vertical anchorage bolts with conical seatings, and the rear end

is attached to the body frame adjacent to the second main crossmember of the floor by two horizontal anchorage bolts also provided with conical seatings. The two channel side-members of this A-frame are tied by a channel section crossmember, which carries the front-end engine mountings.

The bulkhead support brackets, which are bolted to the frame side-members, are extended downwards in order to provide a pickup for a circular crossmember that forms the rear support of the engine. Additionally, the bulkhead bracket assembly houses the pivots for the steering relay levers.

The attachment of the A-frame to the body is by four 1in (25mm) diameter high-tensile pins located in specially designed brackets on both the frame and the body structure.

The rear subframe, or B-frame, consists of two parallel frame sections that also act as radius arms. They're attached at the front to the body structure through rubber mounting bushes and secured by 1in diameter high-tensile pins to brackets at the third body crossbar. At the rear is a transverse crossmember to which are attached the lower ends of the vertically mounted rear coil springs and dampers, within which are housed the shock absorbers, situated within the wheel-arch boxes adjacent to the rear bulkhead and platform riser.

The side members are holed to allow the rear axle tubes to pass freely through, the rear axle being carried on inclined Metalastik mountings. An intermediate crossmember is fitted forward of the rear axle.

The upper ends of the shock absorbers are attached to and act directly on the wheel-arch boxes via an attachment bracket which is so constructed as to form the retaining spigot seating for the coil spring abutments. In order to take care of side movement of the axle, a Panhard or transverse rod is incorporated in the design of the B-frame. One end is attached to the offside of the axle casing, and the other is attached to a reaction bracket mounted on the nearside of the body structure. Both ends of the transverse rod are provided with flexible rubber bushes. It is accepted that the B-frame and the layout of the coil springs provide torsional stiffness, outstanding ride and an excellent tilt figure that's rarely surpassed by similar vehicles.

A strut is fitted across the open forward ends of the B-frame to resist the tendency for the handbrake linkage to close the members together.

The A-frame and B-frame can be readily detached from the main body structure with their mechanical components attached, so that the whole assembly can be removed for servicing and repair, although this is rarely carried out for the A-frame.

Engine

The AEC AV590 is a 9.6-litre six-cylinder diesel engine mounted longitudinally at the front of the vehicle. The cylinder block and crankcase are cast integrally, and together with the main bearing caps are manufactured

BELOW In the early 1990s TBP Holdings overhauled B-frames as part of the RML refurbishment programme. Here a B-frame is seen from the rear nearside corner. *(Andrew Morgan)*

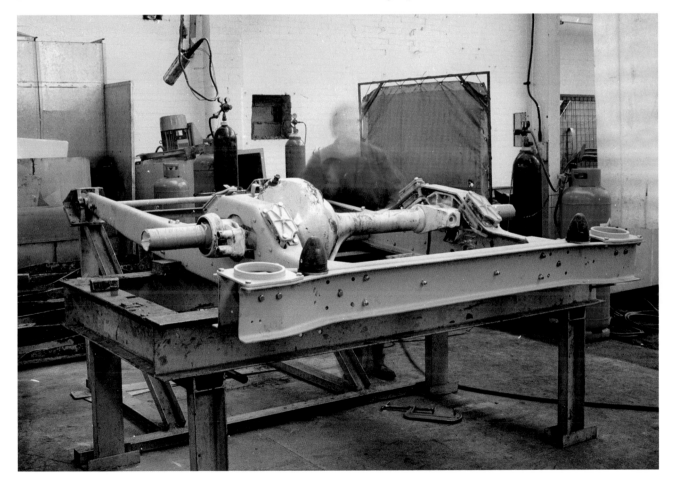

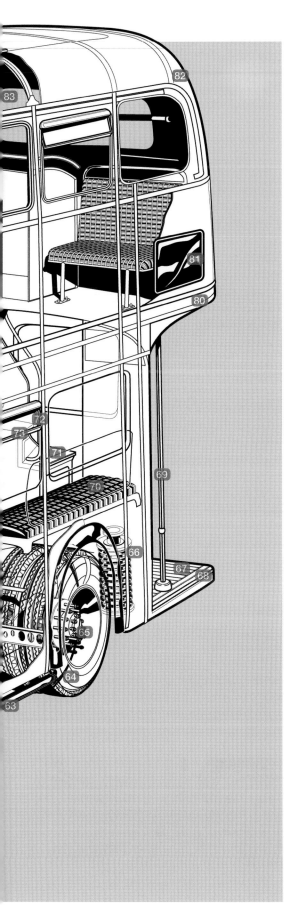

1 Upper windscreen
2 Windscreen wiper arm with wiper fixed to end
3 Driver's emergency window
4 Driver's seat
5 Steering wheel
6 Lower windscreen
7 Gear lever
8 Handbrake
9 Dash board
10 Plate to seal lower windscreen
11 Steering column
12 Panel screw
13 Offside side light
14 Fresh air vent for cab
15 Air vent for cab heater
16 Offside headlight trim
17 Offside head light
18 Offside front wing
19 Offside front tyre
20 Accelerator pedal
21 Brake pedal
22 Radiator grille badge
23 Radiator
24 Radiator grille
25 Engine fan
26 Registration plate
27 Header tank filler cap
28 Air intake
29 Fuel injector
30 Header tank for coolant system
31 Thermostat housing
32 Power steering reservoir
33 Fuel filter
34 Fuel pump
35 Flywheel
36 Nearside headlight
37 Headlight trim
38 Fog light
39 Nearside front wheel
40 Front wheel trim
41 Nearside front hub
42 Bonnet to engine bay
43 Nearside side light
44 Nearside wing assembly
45 Handle
46 Nearside mirror
47 Canopy number blind box with exterior handle to adjust blind
48 Indicator lens in rubber indicator ear
49 Fuel tank
50 Brake pump drive unit, with hydraulic brake pump behind
51 Front prop shaft
52 Compressor
53 Exhaust pipe
54 Exhaust silencer
55 Gearbox
56 Air tank
57 Side arm of rear sub-frame (b-frame)
58 Offside rear spring
59 Axle tube
60 Rear prop shaft
61 Body crossmember
62 Differential
63 "Dog" rail
64 Nearside rear tyre and wheel
65 Nearside rear hub
66 Nearside rear spring
67 Platform
68 Platform nosing
69 Platform pole (nicknamed the monkey pole)
70 Nearside bench seat
71 Staircase
72 Quarter drop side window
73 Winder bar
74 Offside bench seat
75 Electrical cable in conduit
76 Seat frame fixed into floor
77 Seat cushion
78 Seat squab (back)
79 Floor framework structure
80 Relief band
81 Side blind box
82 Rear roof dome
83 Upper deck emergency exit
84 Staircase mirror
85 Staircase outside handrail
86 Seat stanchion
87 Seat frame
88 Seat stanchion
89 Standard position of radio aerial
90 Front roof dome
91 Offside front quarter drop front window
92 Winder bar
93 Nearside front quarter drop front window
94 Nearside front upper deck window (fixed lower half)
95 Offside front upper deck window (fixed lower half)
96 Window pan
97 Offside corner advert panel
98 Route number destination blind box
99 Intermediate destination blind box
100 Nearside corner advert panel
101 Rivet
102 Ultimate destination blind box
103 Beading
104 Top radiator / heat exchanger

from cast iron. The lower half of the crankcase is manufactured from magnesium alloy and incorporates the sump.

Push-fit wet cylinder liners are fitted, sealing at the crankcase end being effected by two synthetic rubber rings housed in grooves machined in the cylinder block. At the top end, a register on the cylinder liner locates in a recess in the cylinder block and provides a metal-to-metal joint.

A separate compartment is formed at the front of the engine block that houses the timing gears. The crankshaft gear drives a solid idler wheel above it, with which the camshaft and fuel injection pump driving gears mesh. The drive for the water pump is taken from the camshaft gear via a second idler gear. The pressure oil pump is located in the front main bearing cap and is driven directly by the crankshaft gear. The scavenge oil pump is mounted directly beneath and in line with the pressure pump and is driven by the pressure pump gear.

The crankshaft is drop-forged and is carried in seven main bearings which are of the precision, thick steel-shell type, copper lead lined, and flashed with a coating of lead-tin. The shaft is unhardened and incorporates an oil wind-back scroll and rubbing strip-type rear oil seal. The front oil seal is of the conventional spring-loaded rubber type. At the front end of the shaft is keyed a three-groove 'V' pulley that provides the belt-drive for the alternator.

The camshaft is of cast iron with all cam surfaces chill-hardened. It is supported in the crankcase by seven plain bearings. The front bearing is of phosphor bronze and the remainder are of the steel-backed, tin-based babbit type which, being larger than the cams, permit easy assembly of the shaft. The camshaft has a hardened stud screwed into its front end that's adjacent to the cover plate, the end float of the camshaft being controlled by shims in conjunction with the cover plate. The cover plate itself is retained in position by three set bolts and two clamping plates.

The camshaft gear is provided with three unevenly spaced keyways; the correct valve timing is obtained by selecting the appropriate keyway when fitting the gear.

The two detachable cylinder heads are of cast iron and are interchangeable. Each head covers three cylinders and is fitted with renewable valve guides and valve seat inserts. The injectors are fitted in copper sheaths that are in direct contact with the water. Water connection between the two cylinder heads is made by means of a bridge-piece casting fitted to the nearside of the heads.

The heads are tightened down by means of studs and nuts. Two dowels per head are provided for accurate location.

The valves are of the overhead poppet type, operated from the camshaft through flat-faced piston-type tappets – which are slightly offset to equalise wear – and tubular pushrods. Both the inlet and exhaust valves have chromium-plated stems and stellite-faced seatings. Each inlet valve incorporates a mask to promote air swirl and is prevented from rotating by means of a male key on the stem engaging with a slot in a collar dowelled to the cylinder head.

The rocker gear is of conventional design with ball-ended adjusting screws.

The air intake manifold is of cast aluminium and is bolted to the offside of the cylinder heads. The manifold is made in two halves connected by means of a short sleeve, the joint being sealed by a cork ring and jubilee clip. Crankcase breathing is effected through a casting attached to the front rocker cover, which terminates at a small outlet adjacent to the air intake. Crankcase fumes are thus inhaled by the engine induction.

The exhaust manifold is fabricated from steel tubing and is manufactured in two sections connected by a short sleeve to allow expansion to occur freely.

The lubrication system is of the combined pressure and splash type. Oil is supplied to the engine by means of a gear-type pump housed in the front main bearing cap, which draws it through a gauze filter from the main sump at the front of the engine.

The main bearings are fed through a gallery drilled in the engine casing and through oilways communicating with each bearing. The connecting rod big end bearings receive oil under pressure through oilways in the crankshaft, whilst the small end bearings and cylinder walls are splash lubricated.

An external oil filter was originally incorporated in the pressure circuit, which was then removed after the first oil change period and replaced by a bridge piece. Many engines have had the oil filter refitted in later life.

Oil pressure is controlled by means of a spring-loaded pressure relief valve, the adjuster for which is located just in front of the base plate on the sump. Adjustment is carried out by removing the metal cover and locking plate, thus exposing a square-headed shaft. Oil pressure is increased by clockwise rotation.

Engine cooling is effected by the normal fan and water-circulating pump. Various different types of fan have been used and they're mounted directly on to the front of the crankshaft pulley. The water pump is mounted on the offside of the engine and is gear-driven from the timing case.

The engine is mounted on four rubber-bonded sandwich-type mounting pads. The front mounting pads are located between the front crossmember and the engine header tank and are arranged in inverted 'V' form.

The rear mounting pads are attached to the tubular rear crossmember and are arranged in a fairly widely spread 'V' form. Each rear mounting consists of two sandwich units bolted either side of a rigid metal tongue welded to the crossmember. The engine is held down on its mountings by four long bolts that screw into the engine.

The main purpose of the fluid flywheel is to transmit the engine torque or output to the transmission. It doesn't multiply the torque, which is the function of a torque converter, and therefore the fluid flywheel gives a more gentle acceleration.

The fluid flywheel consists of two basic parts, a rotor and the spinner. Each has a series of radial vanes, with one having a greater number than the other. The rotor is connected directly to the engine, and when it rotates the oil in the unit is directed radially in an outward direction, which transfers it to the spinner, causing it to rotate. Connected to the spinner is an output shaft connected via a cardan shaft to the transmission passing through the rotor, supported on a ball bearing. To prevent any leakage externally a face-type seal is fitted, known as the Llewellyn gland. This consists of a floating face seal using bronze and steel for the rubbing surfaces.

The spigot shaft on the rotor is supported on the end of the engine crankshaft by a roller race, the inner and outer runners of which must be kept as a mated unit. The flywheel is marked to

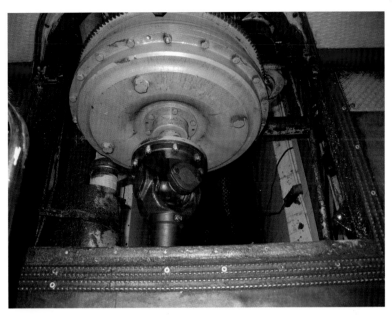

indicate top dead-centre position and the starter rack is attached by ten setscrews to the engine half of the casing. Provision is made for alternative positioning of the rack and for its reversal.

The cardan couplings are of the needle roller bearing type (Hardy Spicer). Each spider of the universal joints is fitted with a grease nipple to lubricate the needle roller bearings. The sliding ends are fitted with grease nipples for lubricating the splines.

ABOVE The J156 fluid flywheel is essentially the same as that employed on the post-war AEC Regent III RT and AEC Regal IV RF types, and incorporates an improved design of Llewellyn gland. It is viewed here from inside the passenger saloon. *(Mark Kehoe)*

LEFT A fixed pointer is positioned on the rear of the engine, and the outer diameter of the flywheel is marked at top dead centre (TDC) with one-inch markings before the TDC position. This is used for valve timing and setting up the fuel pump. *(Mark Kehoe)*

LEFT The starter motor pinion engages with the starter rack on the front of the flywheel. *(Mark Kehoe)*

RIGHT The radiator is mounted on the two projections of the channels forming the A-frame in front of the crossmember that acts as a support for the forward end of the engine. *(Mark Kehoe)*

RIGHT The header tank is separate from the radiator and is mounted on the front of the engine, above the front engine mounting. It's fitted with AC Delco combined filler cap and pressure relief valve (4psi). The thermostat housing is bolted to the nearside of the header tank. *(Andrew Morgan)*

RIGHT The heat exchanger is situated in the centre of the front of the vehicle just beneath the destination blinds and is covered by the hinged grille. The blind is visible in the midway position. *(Mark Kehoe)*

RIGHT With the canopy panels removed, the Ranco valve can be seen. This is operated by the cable visible on the underside, from the control lever at the front of the lower passenger saloon. *(Brian Lewer)*

Cooling system

The radiator is a 'still' tube block type or fin-and-tube block type; both provide a large cooling area and have the good heat transfer qualities needed for this sort of installation. The small top and bottom tanks on the radiator are manufactured from brass. A drain cock is fitted on the bottom of the radiator at the outlet connection.

A cowl is fitted to the engine side of the radiator to guard against injury by the engine fan blades, which extend below the radiator bottom, and to improve the airflow through the tube block. The whole unit is mounted on the front of the side-members of the A-frame by means of brackets and rubber mountings, together with a tie rod between the bottom nearside of the radiator and the side frame.

The cab heater is mounted in front and to the nearside of the steering column. It's enclosed in a metal box that has warm air outlets at the top and bottom. The bottom outlet is a few inches above cab floor level, while the top outlet is ducted across the width of the windscreen at its bottom, and provides the windscreen demisting system. The heater is of the conventional type and relies on an electric fan to provide air circulation. To operate the heater, a lever situated to the left of it must be placed in the down position. This will open the air inlet in the front of the cab, and will at the same time, by making contact with a switch, bring the circulating fan into operation. This then provides fresh warm air heating. Hot water for the cab heater is piped to it from the thermostat housing, and returned via a 'Y' junction in the thermostat bypass pipe close to the water pump.

Saloon heating is achieved by passing ram air from the front of the vehicle over a heat exchanger through which engine cooling water is circulated, and by ducting the warm fresh air to both upper and lower passenger saloons.

Engine outlet water is piped to the heat exchanger from the engine thermostat housing. The pipe runs along the side of the driver's cab and then turns vertically towards the upper saloon. It continues up and then along the inside of the canopy to the Ranco valve or thermostatic control unit located adjacent to the saloon heating radiator. Access to this is via a hinged flap in the canopy panel. The supply pipe passes from the Ranco unit to the heat exchanger. The return pipe from the upper connection on the heat exchanger returns down the offside of the engine and on to a connection on the water pump.

For the 1990s RML refurbishment programme, and on some RMs in subsequent programmes, the upper and lower saloons were fitted with body-side mounted twin pipe convector heating units manufactured by Clayton, and the heat exchanger was removed.

Fuel system

Two types of fuel pump were originally fitted and these are interchangeable. They're the CAV 'N' type and the Simms 'BN' type, and both have a two-speed mechanical governor. Both also have a separate stop control, operated by an Arens cable terminating in a switch unit in the driver's cab.

These pumps have flat bases and are attached to the platform by four setbolts, two short ones at the feed pump side and two long ones at the rear (against the engine block face). The fuel inlet is halfway along the rear face, which on the CAV pump communicates with an internal block felt filter, whilst the Simms pump has a fine gauze strainer in the adaptor.

The main difference between the two types is in length, the Simms pump being 19mm longer than the CAV pump from the front locating bolt to the forward end of the camshaft. In order to make the two units interchangeable on the engine the coupling units are so designed as to take up this difference. The centre assembly, as far as the flange of the short coupling shaft, is permanently attached to the fuel pump flywheel, which remains with the pump.

The fuel injectors are of the multi-hole type with an increased body length to suit the depth of cylinder head, and are otherwise identical with those used on the AEC Regent III RT bus. A small gauze filter is fitted in the injector body by means of an adaptor.

Fuel oil is drawn from the main tank on the offside of the body by the lift pump mounted on the nearside of the fuel injection pump. From the lift pump, fuel is pumped up to the fuel filter, which is a cloth type mounted on the nearside front of the engine. Fuel from the filter is piped

via a screw-type fuel control cock (tap) to the fuel pump. The lift pump is of the diaphragm type and is cam-driven from the fuel pump camshaft. It delivers fuel at 5psi and is provided with a hand-priming lever. A small air vent valve is fitted to the top of the fuel filter with a pipe leading into the injector dribble gallery pipe. This pipe is carried down the rear end of the engine, and from there runs parallel with the feed pipe back to the main fuel tank. Flexible rubber pipes are inserted in both feed and dribble pipes

TOP Simms inline fuel pump. *(Mark Kehoe)*

ABOVE CAV inline fuel pump. *(Andrew Morgan)*

LEFT CAV rotary fuel pump. *(Mark Kehoe)*

between the engine and the A-frame to allow for any relative movement between them.

The standard fuel tank for the RM and RML is of rectangular section and has a capacity of 29 gallons. It's mounted on the underside of the body on the centre of the offside, immediately below the floor, by means of quick-release straps. Detachable covers are fitted to the tank to facilitate cleaning once removed from the vehicle.

The dribble return is discharged into the top of the tank, and the feed pipe is extended to take its supply from a well of approximately two pints capacity in the bottom of the tank. This well is designed to ensure that there's always fuel at the feed pipe regardless of the attitude of the vehicle. A drain plug is fitted in the bottom. The tank baffles are manufactured from perforated sheet to provide added protection against the ingress of foreign matter into the compartment from which the fuel feed is taken.

Exhaust system

The standard steel exhaust system consists of eight sections of piping and a silencer (with one additional section for the longer RCL, RMF and RML types). The first section drops from the engine exhaust manifold to a point on the nearside of the A-frame, where it's joined to a short section of flexible metallic tubing. The third pipe section runs for a short distance parallel to the front frame after its junction with the flexible pipe. It turns across towards the offside, then turns again, passing through a main body crossmember towards the rear of the vehicle. The fourth section, which is also of flexible metallic tubing, connects the third section to the inlet side of the silencer and also passes through a body crossmember. The next section is the silencer, which is positioned between two body crossmembers and is of the Burgess three-pass type. The tail pipe is taken from the rear end of the silencer. It's in four sections and includes a further section of flexible tubing; the final section turns to the offside and is open to the air a short distance behind the rear wheel.

The silencer is held in position at the front end by a strap bolted to the cross-strut between the two arms of the rear axle unit. At the rear end, the fifth section of piping is bolted to a body crossmember close to the end of the silencer. The silencer is easily removed by disconnecting its two four-bolt flanges and the supporting strap.

The whole exhaust system is clipped and fixed throughout its run, and junctions are fitted with spigot sealing joints. No part of the system is lagged but grease shields are fitted in the vicinity of the fluid flywheel and at the front and rear of the gearbox adjacent to the cardan shaft joints.

Some vehicles have been fitted with stainless steel exhaust systems for a far greater life. In the later years of Routemaster regular service, vehicles in London were fitted with particulate traps at the rear of the first section of exhaust under the floor behind the front bulkhead.

Transmission

The Routemaster is fitted with a fully automatic gearchanging system, the operation of which depends on the actual (road) speed. The road-speed sensitive element consists of an alternator (known as the speed sensitive generator, or SSG) driven from the rear of the gearbox, so that this unit has no connection whatsoever with the throttle gear.

The D182 gearbox is of direct selection epicyclic type, controlled by electro-pneumatic valves. It's carried entirely by the body floor frame bars on the underside of the vehicle, on three-point rubber mountings, and is

BELOW Sectional drawing of the D182 gearbox. *(London Transport)*

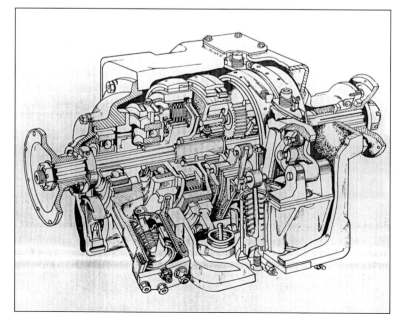

located centrally between the second and third crossmembers. Provision is made for fully automatic operation of second, third and top gears. The SSG is incorporated at the rear end of the gearbox to supply a signal corresponding to road speed, whilst originally a throttle switch was fitted to indicate the throttle pedal position; both communicated electrically to the control panel, which is located behind the removable panel behind the driver's head in the cab.

For the operation of the gearbox, an air pressure system is fitted to operate the brake bands. This consists of a compressor, belt-driven from the gearbox, feeding a single chamber reservoir reducing through a fixed reduction valve to the electro-pneumatic (EP) block on the gearbox. The gearbox is always disengaged when there's no air in the system.

The fundamental difference with this gearbox compared to previous installations is that during a gearchange constant drive is obtained, ie at no time is the engine disconnected from the road wheels. The electrical gear control lever, mounted on the nearside of the steering column, is direct operating, and there's no clutch, operating or speed-change pedal. (A vehicle with two-pedal control is known as being semi-automatic.)

The gearbox doesn't operate by the usual single cylinder and bus bar linkage mechanism. Instead each gear brake band is operated by an independent air piston and cylinder. Top gear is engaged by the actuation of a piston rod (of its

LEFT The speed sensitive generator (SSG). *(Mark Kehoe)*

cylinder unit) on a bell crank lever, which pivots a trunnion ring carrying the top-speed clutch pressure ring.

The admission and release of compressed air to and from the gearbox is regulated by five electro-pneumatic (EP) valves grouped together in a dustproof and waterproof block attached to the offside of the gearbox.

When a gear is engaged the solenoid of the appropriate gear is energised from the circuit completed by the gearchange lever contacts. When the coil of the solenoid is energised the valve lifts and air is admitted to the cylinder of the gear selected. Restrictor valves are incorporated in the adaptors fitted to the base plate of the gearbox cylinders. These restrictors regulate the build-up and fall away of air pressure in the cylinders, such that when a gearchange is made the engaged band releases as the next gear brake band is applied. Hence gear 'overlap' or constant drive is obtained.

LEFT On the offside of the gearbox, the hydraulic brake pump can be seen to the rear of the pump drive unit, with the air compressor below it, and the electro-pneumatic (EP) valve block to the rear of the compressor. Note the filler for the compressor sump can just be seen. *(Mark Kehoe)*

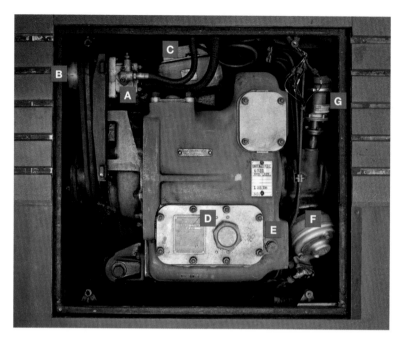

ABOVE Gearbox viewed from the passenger saloon above. *(Mark Kehoe)*

A Hydraulic Plessey brake pump

B Brake pump drive unit

C Electro-pneumatic (EP) valve block

D Gearbox oil filler

E Dipstick

F Speed sensitive generator (SSG)

G Speedometer transmitter

The ratios of the drives are:

Compressor to engine	1:1
Hydraulic brake pump	1.275:1

The speedometer drive is taken from the output shaft bearing housing at the rear of the gearbox by means of a worm and pinion drive, and is fitted opposite the speed sensitive generator.

The gear ratios for the D182 gearbox are:

Top gear	1:1 direct drive
Third gear	1.59:1
Second gear	2.42:1
First gear	4.28:1
Reverse gear	5.98:1

Automatic adjustment of the brake bands is provided for the indirect gears (first, second, third and reverse) by automatic adjusters attached to the pull rods. The top-speed clutch piston rod is of two parts (male and female), and clutch wear is compensated by inserting distance pieces between the abutment faces so that the length of the piston rod is increased.

Lip-type oil seals are fitted to the gearbox case at the input shaft and mainshaft positions.

On the first and reverse gear band assemblies, the automatic adjusters are of the free wheel type, consisting of an adjuster ring, adjuster nut and a specially wound spring. On the second and third gear band assemblies the automatic adjusters are of the cam and roller type.

In both designs the adjuster action causes the adjuster nut and adjuster to be rotated together in a clockwise direction. The action of the automatic adjusters is to maintain a constant clearance between the liner and the drum. The top gear doesn't have automatic adjustment.

Air for the operation of the gearbox is drawn in through a filter unit and passes to the air compressor. The air intake filter is situated in the driver's cab beside the seat; its function is to clean the air entering the air pressure system and to prevent damage to the compressor by foreign matter passing through it.

The air compressor is an air-cooled, horizontal twin-cylinder, single-stage unit of 1¾in (44.5mm) bore x 1⁵⁄₃₂in (29.4mm) stroke, originally manufactured by Clayton Dewandre under licence. The rated output of the compressor is 2.8ft³ (0.079m³) per minute at 2,000rpm at a pressure of 100psi (689.5kPa). The compressor is driven at engine speed.

Air from the compressor is delivered to the unloader valve mounted on the reservoir unit, which is mounted under the nearside of the body. The unloader valve maintains the air pressure within the reservoir at 85–110psi (586.1–758.4kPa).

RIGHT The air compressor. *(Mark Kehoe)*

LEFT At the front of the gearbox, a two-grooved pulley carries two half-inch wedge belts that drive the air compressor and, above it, the hydraulic pump of the brake system. Adjustment of the belt drive is by adjusting the mounting bracket of the brake pump drive.
(Mark Kehoe)

From the unloader valve the air passes to the air reservoir. The original reservoir is a single compartment made of heavy welded plate of 435in³ (7,128.3cm³) capacity, where it's stored for use only in gearchanging. It consists of a cylindrical shell with a flat plate welded at one end to form a mounting for the unloader valve and reducer valve. The other end is hemispherical and carries a welded boss for a test point adaptor. The drain plug is situated in the middle of the cylindrical section of the tank.

The unloader valve allows the pressure in the reservoir to build up to a maximum of 110psi +/- 5 (758.4kPa +/- 34.5), when it cuts out and allows the compressor to deliver air to atmosphere without compressing it, thereby reducing the amount of work it has to do. The valve cuts in again when the reservoir pressure falls to a value of 85psi +/- 2½ (586.1kPa +/- 17.2).

The reducer valve serves to reduce the air from the reservoir to 60psi +/- 2½ (413.7kPa +/- 17.2), this being the operating pressure of the gearbox. A test point adaptor is fitted on the outlet pipe from the reducer valve, as well as an electro pneumatic switch indicating that the air pressure has fallen below 45psi (310.3kPa). The microswitch in this unit is connected to the red warning light on the warning flag unit mounted in the driver's cab above the top right-hand side of the windscreen. When this light is illuminated as a result of low pressure, the warning arm

normally associated with low brake pressure doesn't operate.

From the reducer valve, the air is fed to the electro pneumatic block mounted on the side of the gearbox.

In order to provide drainage of water from the complete air system, drain points are provided on the main reservoir and on the unloader valve. As well as the filter in the driver's cab, the other filter on the air system is on the unloader valve.

LEFT A new ten-litre air tank, as fitted to the RML fleet when they were refurbished in the early 1990s, complete with new pressure limiting valve to the right.
(Andrew Morgan)

LEFT The gearbox pressure warning switch, which incorporates the microswitch.
(Mark Kehoe)

Steering gear

The steering column is of the worm and nut type with power assistance obtained from a hydraulic ram fitted to the pull and push rod (drag link), the power being derived from an engine-driven Plessey gear-type pump fitted in tandem with the fuel pump. The column is mounted on the offside of the A-frame by bolts located through the steering box projection. A mineral oil is used throughout as the power steering fluid (ie an hydraulic fluid is used).

The oil filler plug is located at the front side of the box and is accessible once the radiator grille has been removed. A drain plug is also fitted.

The steering wheel is secured to the column by a jack nut and key. An AEC-badged cover was originally fitted over the jack nut in the centre.

From the normal drop arm a drag link carries the steering wheel movement to the power-steering jack body. Also attached to this body but further forward is a relay lever that pivots about a point on the outside of the A-frame offside member. Attached to the opposite end of this lever is a short steering arm (side arm) connected to the road wheel, and a track rod connection that relays the steering movement to the nearside of the vehicle in conjunction with a relay lever and short steering arm, etc.

The steering jack body is so arranged that it's free to slide on the combined piston and rod anchored to the inside of the A-frame (offside). Thus there's a mechanical connection between the steering wheel and the road wheels, the power jack only giving assistance to this movement once the steering wheel has been moved.

For the power assistance, hydraulic fluid is drawn from the header tank that's located on the front nearside of the engine behind the oil filler, while suction is through a coarse wire mesh filter. The fluid enters the pump by the inlet part and is fed to the pair of pump gears. The fluid under pressure leaves on the opposite side, feeding to a flow valve.

The purpose of the flow valve is to limit the maximum flow to a desired figure. As the pump speed increases so the pump flow tends to rise. As the pump has to give a satisfactory flow at idling, the full flow at maximum speed would tend to make pipe sizes excessively large. When the flow pressure exceeds a designed figure the pressure overcomes the spring load and the piston slides to the right, allowing a port to communicate with the suction side of the pump. Thus the surplus flow returns direct to the pump.

The piston of the power jack is made of aluminium alloy and is fitted with a cast iron piston ring seal. As oil pressure is applied on both sides of this piston separately, oil seals are provided where the valve body slides over the piston rod.

In the valve body a bobbin valve is fitted. This is spring-loaded to return it to the central position, and provides in addition a minimum load figure beneath which assistance isn't obtained. This makes the Routemaster comparable with other vehicles in unladen condition.

The oil previously on the other side of the piston is free to flow into the return pipe via the other cross-drilling in the bobbin, into a groove in the bobbin that's in communication with the return. The reverse movement of the bobbin will cause the piston to move in this direction by a similar chain of events.

Axles and suspension

Instead of leaf springs as fitted to the RT, the Routemaster employs coil springs with telescopic shock absorbers at each wheel position.

The front suspension is of the wishbone type with independent coil spring suspension and is fitted with hydraulic shock absorbers mounted centrally inside the coil springs.

In the Routemaster, the usual axle beam is replaced by a box member of welded construction that's bolted to the outside of the frame members and is known as the 'boat'. To the top and bottom ends of the boat are attached the wishbone assemblies, which consist of unequal-length paired arms pivoted on the front axle boat member. The kingpost carrying the stub-axle assembly joins the outer ends of the wishbone assemblies. The vertical load is taken by the thrust buttons situated at the bottom of the kingpin. The pivots, wishbone and swivel pin bosses are carried in preloaded conical rubber bushes.

The coil spring and shock absorber are mounted at the bottom end on the underside of the lower wishbone link and at the top end on the front axle boat member. Rubber bump and rebound stops are fitted to the lower and upper links contacting the stop brackets formed by the main front axle member or suspension member.

The hub lubricant is by lip-type seal. Contamination of the brake liners by grease is prevented by a conical metal shield mounted to the brake carrier. This shield mates with a dished shield attached to the hub flange.

The standard rear axle is a conventional differential of the spiral bevel type 5.22:1 ratio, with fully floating axle shafts. The steel axle casing is of the usual banjo shape and is carried by rubber Metalastik mounting pads (known as sandwich rubbers), arranged in inverted vee formation, bolted to the longitudinal members of the rear B-frame. This allows relative movement of the wheels but increases roll stiffness and resists axle wind-up. The frame members are so shaped that the axle tubes pass through large holes in the B-frame side members, the hubs, etc, being mounted on the outside.

Originally a bellows gland oil seal was fitted to the hubs whilst a lip-type oil seal was fitted to the input coupling of the differential. At a later date lip-type oil seals were fitted in place of the bellows and in consequence an additional protection seal was fitted between the inboard bearing and the differential.

In the case of the rear suspension unit, coil springs and shock absorbers are used to support the rear end of the two channel members forming the rear B-frame unit. The whole unit is pivoted at its front end on brackets adjacent to the third body cross-bearer. Between the two channel section members at the rear end is a transverse member that extends behind the rear wheels to the extremity of the body. At its outer end are fitted the shock absorbers and coil springs, which locate at the upper end in the body beneath the longitudinal seats. The distance between spring centres corresponds to the wheel track, thus giving greater stability than the orthodox leaf springs mounted inboard of the wheels.

Rubber bump stops are fitted to restrict maximum movement of the B-frame in both directions.

Lateral movement of the axle is resisted by a Panhard rod between the offside of the rear

axle unit and the nearside of the body structure at the nearside rear wheel arch. A Metalastik Spherilastik bearing is included at one end and an Ultra duty bush at the other.

The shock absorbers differ in respect of size front to rear, and each make functions on its own principle. Therefore vehicles should be fitted with a common make of shock absorber all round. However, each make is interchangeable position for position, with each having similar performance.

The rear suspension on RMC, RCL and BEA/ RMA types was originally constructed with air suspension. However, after problems with the pipework, valves and air bags, or simply a lack of spare parts, many have been replaced with standard coil springs.

RIGHT The brake drum is carried out on the wheel studs being secured by two setscrews. The adjustable anti-squeak band that's often fitted can be clearly seen.
(Andrew Morgan)

ABOVE A rear brake drum is visible once both wheels have been removed.
(Andrew Morgan)

RIGHT An early photograph illustrates the removal of the brake drum and wheel hub assembly to show the brake and the 'S'-shaped cam.
(RM8 Club)

Brake gear

The foot brake is hydraulically operated and controlled by means of a foot brake valve. The front brake cylinders are mounted on the back plate and the piston rod from the hydraulic cylinder connects directly to the combined brake camshaft lever/slack adjuster.

The rear brake cylinders are mounted inside of the side-frame members to the rear of the brake camshaft. The piston rod connects directly with the camshaft lever.

The Routemaster is fitted with fixed cam, fixed anchor leading and trailing brake shoes. To compensate for the differing radii of the two shoes, the leading shoe was originally fitted with a moulded lining and the trailing shoe with a higher friction woven lining. This helped to balance out the level of the brake force and provided a balance of wear between the liners. More recently non-asbestos moulded linings have been fitted at all positions.

The brake camshafts carrying 'S'-shaped cams are mounted in needle roller bearings and operate the brake shoes, mounted on fixed pivots, through rollers. The rollers are fitted in the nosepiece of each brake shoe, with three sizes available – 1½in to 2in in diameter (38–51mm) – according to the brake drum diameter in use, between 10in and 10.25in (254–260mm), in order to wear the

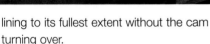
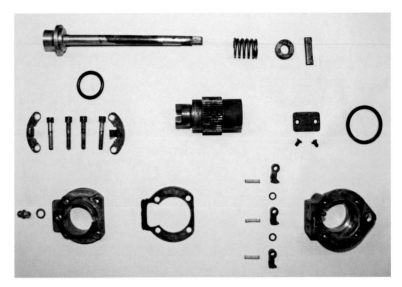

lining to its fullest extent without the cam turning over.

The front linings are 4¾in (120.6mm) wide whilst the rear linings are 7¾in (196.8mm), both being ¾in (19.1mm) thick. The linings are affixed by 90° rivets to the shoes. The linings should still be linished or profiled to match the brake drum diameter so that the liner makes best contact (at least 90%) with the drum surface area when the brakes are applied. By this method, the brake drum and shoes become a set.

In each side of the linings a small hole is drilled at the appropriate spot to indicate the point of maximum wear. The rule of thumb is that once the hole has been broken into, the brake shoe needs to be replaced within 2,000 miles.

The Routemaster was fitted with ratchet and pawl (RP) automatic brake adjusters from 1963 onwards; previously manual adjusters had been fitted. The mechanism operates to rotate the brake camshaft relative to the brake lever, so that as lining wear takes place the lining-to-drum distance remains constant.

The handbrake lever assembly is mounted on a needle roller bearing assembly surrounded by a casting that's bolted to the inside of the offside member of the A-frame. The shape of the lever is such that it's carried to the left-hand side of the driver instead of the right-hand as

ABOVE LEFT With the exhaust removed, this refurbished B-frame can be seen with new sandwich rubbers and no gaps around the flitch plates. The brake adjuster and wheel cylinder have been refitted.
(Andrew Morgan)

ABOVE Brake adjuster dismantled.
(Brian Lewer)

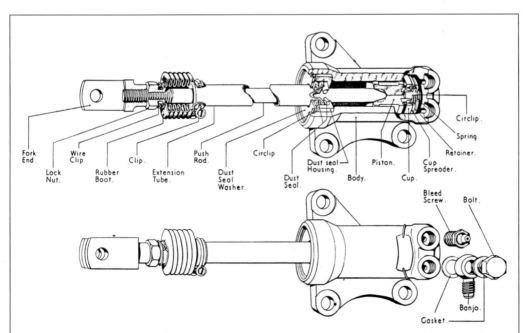

LEFT Wheel cylinder.
(Lockheed)

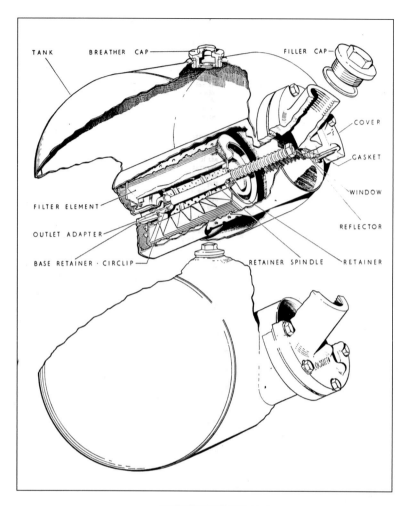

on previous London bus types. The pawl and quadrant are not fitted with an oil bath. The pawl is of the trailing type.

The handbrake effort is carried by rod from the main lever just above the pawl pivot to a swing lever mounted on the A-frame side-member. A further rod takes it to a relay bracket where a branch leads to the nearside of the vehicle. Here another, similar relay bracket is mounted. The handbrake rods then continue separately from each relay bracket to each rear wheel and brake camshaft lever.

Braking system

The hydraulic brakes are normally of Lockheed design, with the front and rear brakes operated by separate valves through a single brake pedal. Adequate braking reserve is provided by two piston-type accumulators, and continuous flowing braking is available on both lines once the accumulators are fully charged from the transmission-driven hydraulic pump. It's important to note that a mineral oil is used throughout as the brake fluid (*ie* an hydraulic fluid is used, *not* a brake fluid). All of the hydraulic brake equipment is attached to the underside of the body structure.

The Routemaster hydraulic braking system combines the separate accumulators for front and rear wheel braking and maintains a continuous flow circuit once the accumulators have been charged. The hydraulic system is only used for braking purposes, as the gearbox has its own separate air pressure system and the power-assisted steering is supplied by a separate engine-driven pump.

The fluid is drawn through a filter from a header tank mounted on the offside of the vehicle to a Plessey gear-type hydraulic pump mounted on the front end of the direct-acting

ABOVE Brake system header tank. *(Lockheed)*

RIGHT Header tank viewed from open flap behind the offside front wheel. *(Mark Kehoe)*

FAR RIGHT The hydraulic brake pump (to the left) and the pump drive unit (to the right). *(Andrew Morgan)*

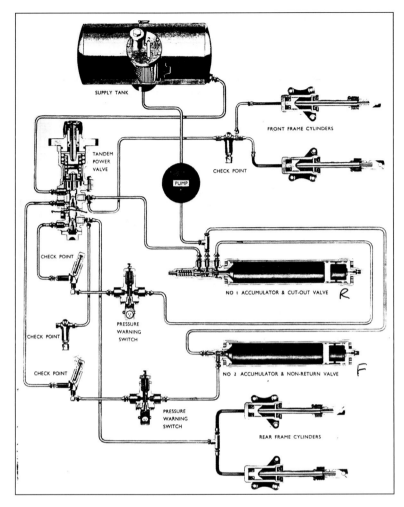

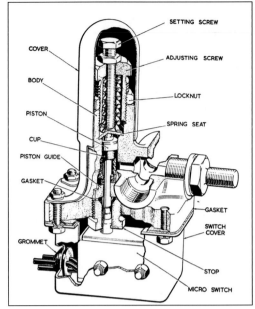

ABOVE Brake pressure warning switch. (*Lockheed*)

LEFT Diagrammatic layout of brake system. (*Lockheed*)

gearbox, being driven by two belts in tandem with an air compressor for the gear system. (The pump is protected from the belt load by a drive housing that's driven by the belts; the quill drive connects the drive housing to the pump.) It's then fed to the non-return valve mounted on the front brake accumulator (No 2), and also to the cut-out valve on the rear brake accumulator (No 1). Thus both accumulators build up together.

In each of the accumulator hydraulic supply lines to the respective brake valves there are pressure warning switches, which are electrically connected to a low-pressure warning flag unit and white warning lamp in the driver's cab.

Once the accumulators have been charged, and after the cut-out valve has operated, the pump delivery is still fed through the cut-out valve leaving at the other port, and passes through the brake valve and hence to the header tank. Thus when the brake pedal is depressed the back pressure of the pump in the continuous-flow circuit is available for braking, and any make-up to balance the pedal load is available from the accumulators.

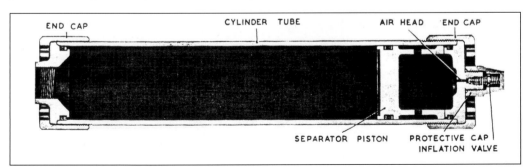

LEFT Lockheed accumulator. (*Lockheed*)

A common return pipe from the tandem brake valve completes the continuous-flow circuit, as well as the exhausting of fluid to the header tank after releasing the brakes.

With this tandem system the maximum possible safety is obtainable in the case of a brake-line failure, as both front and rear braking systems are entirely independent after the accumulators.

Test points for front and rear line pressure are incorporated on the front axle boat, so that a pit isn't necessary for access. Additional test points are fitted for accumulator pressure on the inside of the A-frame. These test points have a needle valve seating, so the fluid pressure can only be recorded once the needle valve is released by unscrewing. This enables gauges to be fitted without first destroying hydraulic pressure.

The brake valve, or tandem power valve, is directly operated by the foot-brake pedal and is carried on a three-bolt fixing in a bracket attached to the steering column. As the name suggests, it comprises two valves in tandem which control the two entirely separate brake lines equally, if set up correctly.

The purpose of the accumulators is to store a reserve of fluid under pressure to provide the potential either to make up the continuous flow for the brake-line pressure, or to operate the brakes should the pump not be charging. Routine maintenance is generally confined to checking the air pre-charge pressure and recharging as necessary.

Should the hydraulic pressure in either accumulator fall below the desired minimum the appropriate warning switch will be de-energised, the warning 'STOP' flag will drop and the white lamp will illuminate on the low-pressure indicator fitted above the top right-hand side of the windscreen.

The accumulator consists of a steel cylindrical shell fitted with removable end caps. Inside is a piston with seals at either extremity. Air is introduced on one side by means of a Schrader valve, whilst fluid is introduced on the other. When hydraulically discharged the piston is at the end of the cylinder and air occupies the entire volume. The pressure of the air under these conditions is 450–500psi (3,102.7–3,447.5kPa).

When the fluid is introduced by the pump it forces the floating piston towards the opposite end of the cylinder, at the same time increasing the air pressure. When the piston reaches the opposite end of the cylinder the air pressure is approximately 1,250psi (8,618.7kPa) and the cylinder may be said to be fully charged. It's then that the cut-out valve operates and passes the fluid to the continuous-flow system.

Electrical equipment

The electrical system operates at a nominal 24V, and a two-wire (insulated return) system is used throughout. Earth-return components aren't used because of the risk of electrolytic corrosion, and no specific earth current paths are provided around the vehicle.

Two alternative manufacturers of electrical equipment were fitted for the charging and transmission components, namely Simms and CAV.

Cables are run through PVC plastic conduits, except under the floor and engine bay where aluminium conduits are used with appropriate junction boxes etc. Heavy cables and certain light flexibles are of stranded aluminium; the remainder are stranded copper. The only exception for heavy cables is in the battery compartment, where stranded copper is used for alkaline battery connections. All insulation is PVC.

Colour combined with letter-coding was devised to identify circuits. Positive and negative feeds to switch and fuse panels were in red and black, but each panel had its own individual cable colour for the sub-circuits. Marking of terminal posts was by letters, while cables from them were marked with the letter and, in addition, were numbered progressively, ie a terminal post marked 'A' has cables from it marked A1, A2 etc.

Unified threads have been used extensively for mounting of panels and panel covers, etc, and BA and BSF threads have normally been used in the assembly of the panels.

Crimping of ferrules, ring-tongue terminals and lugs was adopted in preference to soldering. The crimping configurations are of two types, hexagonal for heavy cables and indented for light cables. This method of fixing required no special skill, and extreme care is necessary when stripping back any insulation, as it's essential you don't sever or nick any of the strands. Only a suitable corrosion inhibitor should be used for aluminium/aluminium connections, so as to prevent oxidisation from taking place when a joint is crimped.

The only soldered connections are those on the heavy copper flexible leads used in conjunction with alkaline batteries.

Alternator

Some Routemasters were originally constructed with DC generators and control panels. However, these were replaced by AC equipment during their operational lives with London Transport.

The CAV alternator is a totally enclosed three-phase, twelve-pole unit, 8in, 7in or 203mm diameter according to the model, mounted in an adjustable cradle attached to the offside forward end of the engine crankcase and driven directly from the crankshaft by vee belts.

The rotor is of imbricated design, consisting of two six-pole interleaved portions embracing a single field coil on the shaft portion. Excitation current is conveyed through carbon brushes and slip rings. The stator carries a distributed three-phase star-connected winding.

The original rectifier unit comprised two three-phase full-wave rectifiers, one being the main rectifier and the other a small unit supplying the field via the control panel. Both are housed in a ventilated case mounted under the floor on the offside immediately behind the driver's cab. Later alternator types DY36, 37, 39 and 53 (AC203) had built-in rectifiers, and the connections to the external unit are bridged out.

The CAV control panel comprises vibratory regulators for voltage and current control, together with a relay for isolating the cab heater when the engine is stopped. This relay is necessary as there's no cut-out to perform this function. The panel was fitted with a switch for reducing the regulated voltage in summer. The CP13 control panel is a solid-state unit and doesn't have a summer/winter charge-rate switch.

The Simms alternator is a totally enclosed eight-pole three-phase machine, approximately 8in (203mm) in diameter, with imbricated rotor, a single field coil and outboard-mounted slip rings. It's belt-driven at a ratio of 2.52:1 and

is accommodated on the same cradle as the CAV alternator. The rectifier for this unit comprises a full-wave rectifier and a blocking diode in the battery circuit. A heavy-duty resistor is also incorporated in the battery circuit to provide a voltage reference for current control. The assembly is housed in a ventilated case mounted under the floor on the offside immediately behind the driver's cab. The later DY38 alternator has a built-in rectifier, and the external unit is bridged out.

A fully transistorised control was later fitted for both voltage control and current limitation. A blocking diode replaces the conventional cut-out and a zener diode provides the reference voltage for voltage control. The control panel isn't provided with a switch for reducing the regulated voltage and no main fuse is fitted.

Automatic gearbox equipment

Two alternative automatic gearbox control systems were originally used, from two different suppliers, namely Self-Changing Gears (SCG) and CAV, both performing the same function. Some refurbished vehicles had the CAV551 unit fitted from the early 1990s but it should be noted that several variations were used.

The system consists of a control panel, a multi-contact switch (subsequently removed) adjacent to and operated by the throttle pedal, a gear selector on the steering column, an electromagnetic valve unit assembly attached to the gearbox and a speed-sensitive generator mounted on and driven by the output shaft of the gearbox.

The throttle switch is connected via a seven-way plug and socket, and the control panel via a 30-way plug and socket. Connection to the selector switch and gearbox valve assembly is by detachable contact assemblies. The plugs and sockets also serve as points for the insertion of the original test equipment.

In automatic control, with the gear selector in fourth position, second, third and fourth gears only are under automatic control. Upon starting, second gear is engaged from neutral with the first movement of the throttle pedal, subsequent engagement of third and fourth gears being dependent on vehicle speed.

When coasting to a stop with the throttle pedal completely released the engaged gear will be retained down to about 3mph (4.8kph); below this speed neutral will automatically be selected. Subject to the functioning of the speed-sensitive generator, the same feature will apply to first, second and third gears when in manual mode.

In manual control, reverse, first, second and third gears can be manually selected; third gear, however, will only engage when the vehicle is above 3mph. Reverse gear is retained during selection and not disengaged, as are the forward gears, by complete release of the throttle pedal.

Starter motor

The starter motor is operated by a switch on the nearside of the header panel in the driver's cab through a solenoid attached to the commutator end of the starter. (This will only operate if the Arens stop switch has been fully pushed in.) The drive is transmitted by a pinion to a steel rack on the periphery of the flywheel. The hook-type starter switch was replaced with a rotary switch as part of the early 1990s RML refurbishments. A security device was also fitted which involved the insertion of a key or fob before the starter switch could be activated.

This starter motor, coded SM14, was used on all AEC and Leyland-engined Routemasters and can also be found on other London Transport bus types up to the 1980s.

Batteries

Both lead acid and alkaline batteries were originally fitted to Routemasters and the battery crate is designed to accommodate either type in various dimensions. Naturally, however, during their operational life they gradually standardised on alkaline batteries. The batteries are held by means of adjustable diagonal clamping bars, which are covered with a coating of nylon or anti-sulphuric acid paint to prevent corrosion and electrolytic chemical reaction.

The batteries are completely enclosed in a locker. The battery crate has a fibreglass shield on the offside and a fibreglass drip tray under the batteries, while the whole compartment is underskinned with a fibreglass dust shield.

Some vehicles, including most of those that

have been refurbished, have been fitted with battery isolator switches and booster sockets; these are usually located at the bottom of the staircase on the platform.

The batteries are accessible for topping up from inside the vehicle after raising the hinged lid in the luggage area under the staircase. A guard rail is fitted at the front of this lid to prevent luggage from falling out.

The main battery cables and junction block can be accessed by removing the offside longitudinal rear-seat squab.

Lighting equipment

The original lower and upper saloon lighting was provided by nine tungsten bulbs in the lower saloon and 12 in the upper saloon, controlled by a switch and fuse panel situated on the rear bulkhead structure under the staircase. Access to the lighting switch panel is through an opening in the access and stairwell-lining panel adjacent to the top left-hand side of the conductor's locker.

Fluorescent tubes 600mm (23.4in) long were fitted to the interior advert, and also to the saloon lighting of RMA, RMC and RCL vehicles. Refurbishments from the early 1990s onwards saw various types of fluorescent lights being fitted with the most common being the Transmatic lights fitted during the RML refurbishment programme.

The supply to the switch and fuse panel was originally coloured red and black, with feeds to the lamp holders in yellow. Negative feeds in the lower saloon were blue from the nearside cab header switch and fuse panel.

Inspection lamp sockets and front route number box are also supplied from the lighting switch panel. They're unswitched, requiring only a bulb or wander lead to be plugged into the sockets. In circuit with the nearside lower saloon lighting is a bulb illuminating the route number box on the front bulkhead. Inspection lamp sockets are located under the staircase (rear bulkhead) and under the front facia switchboard.

The dash, tail, rear nearside and offside, registration plate, front nearside and offside and platform lamps are supplied and controlled by a switch on the nearside of the cab header.

FAR LEFT The batteries are located on the offside rear of the body beneath the staircase and are accessible by removing the detachable panel. *(Andrew Morgan)*

LEFT The battery cradle is easily removable as a complete unit. *(Mark Kehoe)*

BELOW The switches controlling the saloon lights are located on the offside rear partition header, and are accessible through an aperture in the lining panel under the staircase, to the left of the conductor's locker. *(Andrew Morgan)*

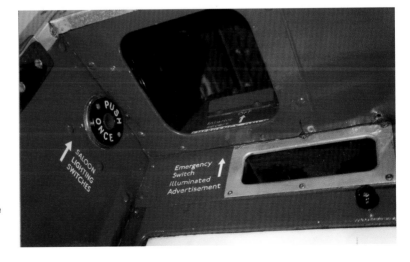

RIGHT The rear registration light can be accessed by opening the flap above the registration plate, and is wired so that it operates with the sidelights. *(Mark Kehoe)*

The stop lamp is supplied and fused by the facia switchboard. It's controlled by a bell switch (also known as a tangent switch) attached to the A-frame and operated by movement of the brake pedal.

The headlamps are supplied and controlled from the facia switchboard located below the indicator switch. The headlamps are further controlled by a floor-mounted dip switch that switches between dip and main beam and is operated by the driver's left foot; the switch is mounted on the nearside front of the cab floor plate. An additional floor switch was mounted on a small pedestal beside the headlamp dip switch to operate the microphone for the radio. In the 1970s radios were fitted to the nearside of the driver's seat together with a microphone and speaker fitted to the nearside cab header, and an aerial was fitted in a round pod on the roof. Although these are by now likely to have been disconnected some of this equipment may still be present, together with lengths of redundant cable. Headlamp bulbs can be replaced by removing the front bezel and releasing the reflector by pressing in and turning the assembly to release it from its keyhole locations.

The fog light, fitted below the nearside headlight, is controlled by a switch on the nearside cab header. The bulb can be replaced by removing the bezel and reflector assembly.

The fog light was often removed in the 1990s either as part of the refurbishment programmes or as a redundant feature.

The direction indicators are supplied and fused by the switch and fuse panel on the nearside cab header and are controlled by a rotary switch mounted on the dash panel. A warning light is situated on the offside corner of the panel and works in conjunction with the switch. The flashing of the indicators and warning light are actuated by an interrupter unit having two sets of contacts, one for the indicators and the other for the warning light. The interrupter unit is mounted behind the cover plate on the nearside cab header.

The front indicators are mounted on the exterior of the vehicle's nearside and offside front, adjacent to the driver's mirrors and level with the relief band. The rear indicators are mounted nearside and offside on the rear panel. The indicators are wired in series, nearside and offside separately.

The driver's cab light, which has its own switch mounted on the lamp cover, is also supplied via the destination lighting switch and is inoperative until the destination bulbs are switched on. It's situated in the top left-hand corner of the driver's cab.

Destination lighting

Originally lighting was fitted to the destination blind boxes as follows:

- Front route number, route and destination box with six bulbs.
- Rear route number, route and destination box with five bulbs.
- Nearside route number, route and destination box with three bulbs.
- Offside route number, route and destination box with one bulb.
- Front bulkhead (under the front canopy) route number box with one bulb.

All bulbs are supplied and controlled from a switch and fuse panel on the nearside cab header. Terminal blocks are used in conjunction with flexible cables at the access doors.

The front bulkhead (under the canopy) route number box is supplied and controlled by the saloon lighting switch panel.

BELOW Destination lighting was originally by standard 24V 12W tungsten bayonet-type bulbs. The later refurbishments had fluorescent tubes fitted instead. *(Mark Kehoe)*

Instruments and switches

The brake and gearbox low-pressure indicator is a typical London Transport unit manufactured by Westinghouse. As well as the solenoid operated 'STOP' flag arm the unit has two warning lamps, white for brake warning and red for gearbox warning. It's positioned in the cab above the windscreen, attached to the front header. If the red warning light or the 'STOP' flag and white warning light are activated, the driver must bring the vehicle to a standstill until the arm disappears upwards and/or the warning light is extinguished (as applicable). Frequent dropping of the 'STOP' flag and illumination of the warning lights indicates a fault in the brake or gearbox pressure systems, in which case the vehicle must be stopped for examination.

The unit is supplied with a fuse on the facia switchboard. The 'STOP' flag arm and white warning lamp are controlled by separate microswitches through a four-way terminal block and operated automatically by the hydraulic accumulators. The flag is actuated by a chain attached to the solenoid. The gearbox warning lamp is controlled by another microswitch operated by the gearbox air system.

The engine Arens stop control is a push-in and pull-out control on the left-hand side of the driver's seat. Its purpose is to shut off the fuel from the pump and to isolate the starter switch, brake and gearbox warning indicator and automatic gearbox circuits, and to eliminate the possibility of draining the battery whilst the vehicle is parked for long periods.

The only other instrument fitted, apart from the direction indicator light, is the speedometer or speedo head. This is located on the dash panel, supplied with a three-phase AC signal from the transmitter. Manufactured by Smith's and designated the 'Electromag', it should always be used with the correct corresponding transmitter (ie with the correctly matched gear to suit the fitted differential). It's illuminated at night by the dash lamp, through slots in the outer casing.

The Electromag embodies a form of commutator that's so connected to the output terminals as to provide sequential pulses of battery current to the indicator head. It's flange-mounted to the gearbox (opposite the speed sensitive generator, mounted on and driven by the output shaft of the gearbox) and connects by a gear mechanism to the main output shaft from the gearbox.

The horn button is on a stem attached to the right-hand side of the steering column. The horn itself is mounted behind the panel that sticks out below the windscreen and above the radiator grille. The horn circuit is supplied and fused by the facia switchboard.

The cab heater is mounted on the dash panel unit on the nearside front of the driver's cab. By depressing the lever marked in white on its right-

LEFT The brake and gearbox low-pressure indicator unit incorporating the 'STOP' flag.
(Mark Kehoe)

CENTRE The Arens stop control switch is attached to the wall between the driver's cab and engine. The engine can't be started until the stop control is fully pushed in.
(Mark Kehoe)

BELOW The speedometer transmitter and standard drive with 11 teeth, to suit the standard 5.22:1 differential.
(Andrew Morgan)

hand side a vent flap opens in the front cab panel and admits fresh air to the radiator. This lever also operates the switch controlling a motorised fan mounted behind the cab heater radiator, and when revolving draws air through it. When depressed the lever on the offside below the dash panel unit opens the other vent flap in the front cab panel and admits fresh air to the cab.

The switch toggle slots for the sidelights, fog lamp, destination lights, headlights and wipers, as well as the cab light and starter switch, are identified by engraved nameplates.

The switches and fuse panel located on the nearside cab header are behind a removable cover plate. A transfer was fixed to the inside of this cover to identify the circuits in the panel.

The switch and fuse panel located on the front facia of the driver's dash are for the headlamps and windscreen wiper. A transfer was fixed to the inside of the cover plate to identify the circuits fused at this panel. A switch box for the driver's assault alarm was later fixed to the bottom of this cover plate. The original 1970s fitment saw all four indicators flashing and the horn sounding when activated. The later 1990s version had an ear-piercing klaxon fitted in the offside bodywork behind the driver's cab.

The signal bell and buzzer are fitted on a common board mounted on the front bulkhead, covered by a panel, behind the driver's head. The buzzer is operated from the upper saloon only by means of a push-button at the top of the staircase. The signal bell is operated by a bell cord running on the underside of the ceiling the length of the lower saloon to a tangent switch mounted on the inside of the front canopy, directly above the engine, and is accessed from the hinged panel. Two push-buttons are fitted on the platform side of the rear bulkhead, one beneath the staircase (for use by the conductor only) and the other on the nearside of the entrance to the lower saloon. The circuits are supplied from and fused at the switch and fuse panel on the nearside cab header.

BELOW A set of body code plates, in this case for an RML.
(Mark Kehoe)

Windscreen wiper

The windscreen wiper motor was originally manufactured by CAV and was a rack type. Mounted on the nearside cab header, it has a rack and pinion-operated flexible drive, which in turn operates another rack and pinion mechanism attached to the top of the windscreen, which operates the wiper arm and blade. The latter is mounted on the outside of the windscreen frame and has a sweep of 150°. The wiper motor body is fitted with a radio and television interference suppressor.

The windscreen wiper is a 14in (356mm) single-blade rubber wiper on an approximately 11in (279mm) arm. Guide wheels were originally fitted to keep the blade the correct distance away from the screen. Windscreen washers were originally only fitted to the BEA front-entrance vehicles fitted with a single-piece windscreen.

The wipers are supplied and controlled from the facia switchboard located below the indicator switch.

Wheels and tyres

Three-piece B6.5 x 20 HD welded-construction wheels were originally fitted with an offset of 5.6in (142mm), and these are fitted with 9.00 x 20/14 PR or 10.00 x 20 radial tyres. At the rear the wheels are fitted in twin formation. Latterly 10.00 x 22.5 radial tubeless tyres have been fitted on 7.5 x 22.5 single-piece wheels, still with a 5.6in offset.

Body

The standard Routemaster (RM) body is of monocoque construction with seating for 64 passengers, and is designed for general ease of routine servicing and maintenance. The bodywork comprises lightweight aluminium alloy sections and sheeting, bolted or riveted together to constitute a strong, rigid, load-carrying structure to which all of the mechanical units are attached.

As no conventional chassis frame is employed, the stressed-skin body structure serves as the main load-carrying element, with single bolt connections for the front and rear mechanical subframe units and gearbox

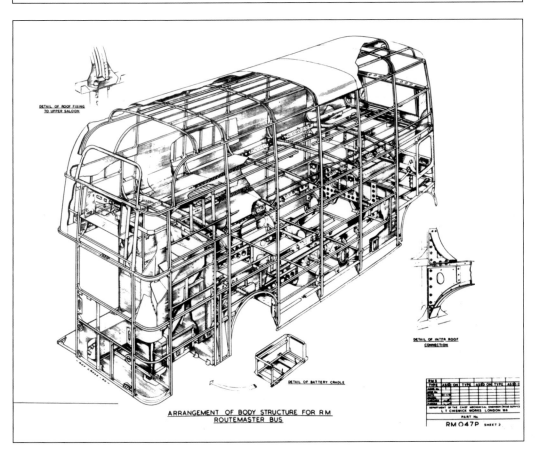

VIEW OF CAB STRUCTURE FROM O/S
FRONT CORNER

FULL SIZE DETAIL SHOWING
FIXING FOR SEAT LEG

FULL SIZE DETAILS AT WAIST
END OF SIDE PILLAR SHOWING
GUN HEADED INSERT BUSHES
FOR SECURING OUTER PANELS

ARRANGEMENT OF BODY STRUCTURE FOR RM
ROUTEMASTER BUS.

RM047.P. SHEET 1 OF 3

DEPARTMENT OF THE CHIEF MECHANICAL ENGINEER (ROAD SERVICES)
L.T. CHISWICK WORKS, LONDON, W4

DETAIL OF ROOF FIXING
TO UPPER SALOON

DETAIL OF INTER ROOF
CONNECTION

DETAIL OF BATTERY CRADLE

ARRANGEMENT OF BODY STRUCTURE FOR RM
ROUTEMASTER BUS

RM047P SHEET 2

DEPARTMENT OF THE CHIEF MECHANICAL ENGINEER (ROAD SERVICES)
L.T. CHISWICK WORKS, LONDON, W4

LEFT Arrangement
of body structure –
rear offside.
(London Transport)

How to build a Routemaster

1 Lower transverse crossmembers.

2 Complete underframe structure.

3 Front bulkhead assembled on a jig.

4 Lower saloon side frame (nearside) is then attached to the underframe.

5 Front of offside rear wheel arch showing stump pillar to bottom of vertical pillar.

6 Lower saloon structure, looking forward from the platform.

7 Lower saloon structure, looking rearwards from front bulkhead.

8 Lower deck ceiling added to side frames.

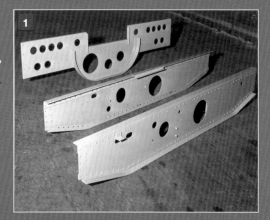

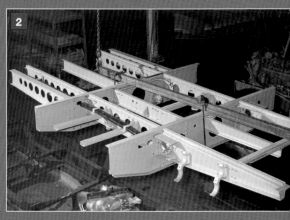

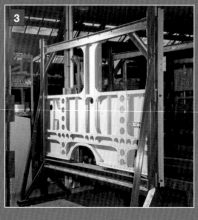

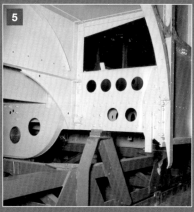

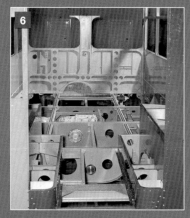

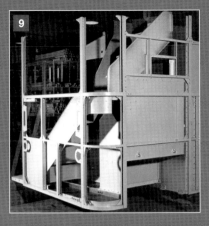

9   Rear platform-area framing.

10 Complete roof from underside.

11 Upper deck assembled separately before being lifted into position.

12 Front subframe (A-frame) complete with AEC AV590 engine.

13 Rear subframe (B-frame) complete with differential.

14 Engine in place and wiring being installed.

15 The front of the body with many parts already painted prior to assembly.

16 The completed vehicle fully finished, windows installed painted, seats added as per the pre-production vehicle RM8.
(All photos RM8 Club)

mountings. A double-skin upper saloon roof is constructed of aluminium sheet and extensions.

The construction uses H-section vertical pillars, with channel-section horizontal connecting rails and corner brackets. Interior panels below the windows in the upper and lower saloons are stress panels and carry all the shear loads in the structure. They're attached to the frame by solid aluminium rivets, and the holes are punch-countersunk to locate the panels into the frame members and provide increased load-carrying capacity.

If a stress panel and/or framing is damaged it must be replaced in an identical fashion, using only grade HE40WP aluminium or its equivalent. Solid rivets are grade NR5; alternatively suitable Monobolts or other blind fixings could be used.

All bolts and screws used in the construction of the Routemaster body, with the exception of 2BA, are of the Unified thread series and are not interchangeable with BSF or Whitworth bolts and screws. The special screws for fixing the flywheel cowl, gearbox trap, front radiator grille and battery valance are of the UNC thread series.

All the exterior panels between the waist and skirt rails on the lower saloon side frames, and between the cantrail and skirt rail on the cab and lower saloon rear frame, are secured

RIGHT Close-up of standard body screw in a piece of body framework, and one screw plus insert loose. *(Mark Kehoe)*

through mouldings (also known as beading) by No 6 UNC special stainless steel (pan-head) screws, screwed into hardened steel insert bushes pressed into the aluminium alloy structural members.

The gutter mouldings over the cab sliding door and the platform canopy valance panel, also the side and rear destination door hinges, are also secured by screws and insert bushes, again for easy replacement.

The remaining exterior panels are fixed by mouldings secured with 'Tucker Pop' hollow rivets, with the exception of the upper saloon roof panel fixings to the hoopsticks, which are riveted with solid aluminium alloy rivets. The Rolls-Royce of aluminium hollow rivets is the nickel-based Monel rivet; these are strong and have a high resistance to corrosion, but they're more expensive and harder to find.

Stainless steel screws (6 UNC) and insert bushes are fitted in the upper saloon roof hoopsticks, longitudinal members and cantrails to facilitate the easy removal of the interior front dome panel, roof lining and lighting panels for the repair of the exterior skin. Screws are also provided around the rear cantrail fixing, but the longitudinal joint of the rear domes is secured with Tucker Pop rivets, since the incidence of damage to the rear domes is considerably less than for the remainder of the roof panels.

The upper corner interior panel and the window top finishers in the lower saloon rear frame are also secured with screws, for easy access to the fixing bolts for the rear frame detachable unit.

All Unified bolts and screws, other than those manufactured in stainless steel, were cadmium plated. Practically all the nuts used were cadmium-plated Simmonds 'Nyloc' types, which are self-locking, require no spring washers and are in the UNF and BA thread series. The main exceptions to the Nyloc are the plain nuts and spring washers used for fixing the bonnet hinge to the fibreglass bonnet, and the UNC locknuts used for the trap fixing screws.

An anchor nut version of the Nyloc is riveted to the body structure for the support of light loads, and similarly doesn't require spring washers. Where a more positive fixing is required brass tapped bosses are used.

Wherever a Hex head bolt or nut is in

contact with aluminium, cadmium-plated plain washers are used, but these aren't required when the bearing is against a steel part.

Spring washers, either the plain Grover type or the countersunk Shakeproof type, are used where there's no other means of locking the thread.

The complete body was designed to be lifted by overhead grab hooks and is built with permanent bracket pads situated at the corners of the front and rear bulkheads to receive these hooks. In addition large-diameter locating pegs are built into the corners to accommodate vertical jacks for lifting and lowering when necessary and for support when the wheels have been removed.

Luggage space is provided above the battery compartment beneath the staircase, as well as a locker and coat-hanging cupboard for the crew.

The rear frame structure to the lower saloon incorporates subsidiary framework for the centrally placed stop light and registration box, twin rear lamps and flashing direction indicators, and is designed as a detachable unit to aid accident repairs. It's suspended from the upper saloon rear frame structure and connected to the rear offside corner rails by bolts and anchor nuts secured to the main structure, with all connections being easily accessible. The top of the platform stanchion has a screw adjustment to suit the height of the canopy.

The main exterior and offside corner panels are designed for replacement without disturbing the rear lights or direction indicators. The bottom corner panel was originally made of aluminium alloy but was subsequently changed to rubber.

The offside rear frame unit originally accommodated the offside illuminated route number box and attachments below the waist for the battery compartment detachable valance. It's bolted and solid-riveted to the upper saloon and lower saloon side frame structure as a semi-detachable unit.

All exterior panels and mouldings below the lower deck windows are secured with stainless steel screws (6 UNC) and hardened steel insert bushes, but are hollow-riveted above this level.

Except for the moulded fibreglass used-ticket box and the lower nearside panel, all interior lining panels and mouldings were originally covered with an artificial leather cloth fabric, known by the brand name Rexine.

The offside corner panel, window finishers and the pillar, waist and cantrail mouldings are secured with stainless steel screws (6 UNC) and insert bushes. Removal of these parts exposes the main fixing bolts that connect the lower saloon rear frame detachable units to the upper saloon rear frame structure.

The platform is constructed of aluminium alloy sections with timber packings on the nearside and rear, originally to accommodate the use of woodscrews for the attachment of platform nosings. The main platform structure consists of extrusions with rolled 'Welsh Hat'-section girders, supporting heavy gauge floor sheeting and skinned on the underside to present a clean finish to dirt and water. The main structure and floor sheets are solid-riveted and the support girders and underskin hollow-riveted.

The flooring is designed in two separate bays, the front with longitudinal girders and the rear bay with transverse girders to prevent rear collision impacts being transmitted beyond the platform.

Bolted to the underside of the platform is a heavy mild steel bracket designed to receive a hook-type rigid towing bar. This was only used within a garage or workshop.

The platform is detachable as a complete unit by means of bolts to connection points at the rear bulkhead, rear frame and rear offside side pillar so that it could be easily replaced after accident damage. It's also supported by the platform stanchion and to a lesser degree the staircase diaphragm.

The staircase is constructed of solid-riveted light alloy sheets and folded or rolled angles, with resin-bonded plywood treads. The main support is a solid-riveted aluminium alloy diaphragm that's bolted to the rear offside side pillar and platform structure. The diaphragm is provided with fixed anchor nuts to facilitate removal of the staircase, to which both the upper and lower inner stringers are connected.

On the luggage compartment side a clip is provided for the conductor's waybill sheets, and on the hidden side of a detachable cover plate there was originally mounted a six-way 'Grelco' terminal block, which when disconnected would isolate all the lower saloon rear frame electrical wiring.

A sheet aluminium alloy locker and coat cupboard for the driver and conductor is provided under the staircase. The conductor's

RIGHT Space is
provided beneath
the staircase for the
conductor to stand
in comfort in the
infamous cubby-hole,
thus allowing for the
unobstructed flow of
passengers entering
or leaving the lower
saloon. *(Mark Kehoe)*

FAR RIGHT The
staircase is designed
in two sections, the
lower section up to
and including No 4
tread being connected
by means of bolts
and anchor nuts for
detachability during
maintenance and
accident repairs. *(Mark
Kehoe)*

locker embodied a base board, shelf and hinged door secured with a budget lock. The door carries a fare-bill card container that's held in position with a 'Gravely' fastener, the door of which is glazed with 26oz toughened glass. Early vehicles had the back of the locker hinged in two sections to provide access to the offside route number box. A receptacle is provided above the locker door to accommodate the conductor's waybill and timecard.

The coat cupboard is positioned between the conductor's locker and the rear bulkhead and contains two coat hooks. The top section of the cupboard door is formed by the fare-table door, but the lower section is hinged separately and arranged to close simultaneously with the fare-table door. The side of the cupboard below the conductor's locker is designed to hinge back clear of the battery locker lid.

Used ticket boxes are fitted to the rear bulkhead and to the lower saloon rear frame at the bottom of the staircase. The handrails on the platform are covered with white-ribbed plastic tape known as 'Doverite'.

The cab is larger than on the earlier RT vehicle and is fitted with a seat having both forward and upward adjustment. It has a sliding door incorporating a quick-action lift-up signalling window that's spring-loaded for ease of use and is a self-contained unit within the window frame. In conjunction with the seal between the steering column and the cab floor plate, the Routemaster was promoted as having a draught-proof cab. A metal container for the driver's time-card was fitted to the offside front at roof level. A time-card

holder was later fitted on the left of the dashboard so that the driver could see his card at all times.

An emergency window is fitted on the nearside; it has interconnected locking handles, one on the inside and the other on the outside of the cab. A small angle-bracket attached to the top of the emergency window frame was originally wired through a hole in the top structure angle to prevent the window from falling out in the event of the catches being accidentally released. The wire used is fine gauge (26 SWG copper), and should be made in one loop only.

A 'finger pull' catch is provided on the front sliding-glass frame to prevent the glass sliding back when the window is in the closed position.

The upper and lower windscreens are independently operated by winding gears, and open outwards hinged from the top. Handles for operating the windscreen are located centrally on the driver's dash panel: the left-hand handle operates the lower half and the right-hand handle the upper half. The top half of the windscreen is fitted with adjustable hinges in order that the rubber seals seat firmly and provide effective waterproofing. The lower windscreen was sealed in later life, including all RMLs that were refurbished in the early 1990s. A single-piece non-opening windscreen was originally fitted to the front-entrance BEA vehicles.

The front centre section of the driver's cab floor is formed by the footplate that's integral with the steering column. Behind the footplate is a hinged trap giving access to the lubricators situated on the throttle cross-shaft, the remainder of the floor plates being fixed to the floor structure by setscrews.

A rectangular mirror is fitted on the cab's offside front pillar, and originally a circular mirror was fitted on the nearside corner of the canopy.

The front destination blind display is similar in appearance to the earlier RT type except that the route number has been transferred to the offside of the box and the blind is smaller in width and depth. A route number blind is fitted in the blind box on the front bulkhead and initially was also fitted in the rear offside route number box. The nearside and rear destination displays are also similar to the RT but vary in overall dimensions.

In order that the driver may adjust the front destination blind without assistance from the conductor, a periscope is fitted on the cab front screen header. A spring-loaded flap is lifted to view the destination blind. The periscope consists of a rectangular-shaped sheet metal box with mirrors placed at the required angles at top and bottom. A winding handle controlling the ultimate destination blind gear (ie the lower blind in the destination box) is located to the offside of the periscope.

For use at night, a folding concertina blind is attached to the nearside front bulkhead behind the driver's seat.

The driver's cab sliding-door mechanism consists of a fixed channel above the doorway for ball-bearing runners attached to the door plate. The bearings were packed with grease on initial assembly. The door is fastened in the open or closed position by a ball catch at each end of the channel working in conjunction with a catch pin on the runner bar attached to the door hanger plate. The bottom of the door is confined within a groove provided with a solid rubber buffer at the front end; this forms a stop when the door is in the open position.

The handbrake steady is fixed at waist level to prevent lever whip.

For greater accessibility, the one-piece nearside front wing structure is a completely detachable unit cantilevered from the front bulkhead on two resilient rubber mountings, and transversely located at the front end by the front crossbrace tube. The electrical wiring is disconnected at the plug and socket.

The wing is designed to conform with the frontal appearance of the vehicle and is constructed in three separate sections, each of solid-riveted aluminium alloys and inter-connected with bolts to enable replacement should the front or rear lower sections suffer accident damage.

The front panel is designed to accommodate the headlight, originally with a cut-out at the bottom edge for the fog lamp. An expanded metal grille was originally fitted to assist ventilation of the front-brake drums.

The bonnet is a double-skin moulded component manufactured from polyester-reinforced fibreglass and attached at its rear edge, via two external hinges, to the bulkhead. When in an open position it's counterbalanced by two spring-loaded articulating arms and is easily removable by the provision of four quick-release pins, two of which are in the hinges and two in the spring-loaded arms. For additional head clearance when the bonnet is opened, a spring-loaded hinged side-flap is provided.

The bonnet is opened by a handle on the nearside. The lock-catch is cable-operated, and is mounted on the underside of the bonnet's front end. The striker bracket of the lock is bolted to the front crossbrace and is adjustable up and down to accommodate any variation in the striker position.

The bonnet catch bracket is mounted on the underside of the front of the bonnet, adjustable fore and aft via slotted holes. The bonnet catch can also be adjusted to obtain correct striking position and alignment of the bonnet. The striker block on the front crossbrace is adjustable up and down and should be positioned so that the bonnet rests on two rubber buffers when the catch is fully engaged.

When the bonnet is closed, two locating blocks on the underside of the front end of the bonnet rest on rubber buffers bolted to the crossbrace. These buffers are adjustable sideways to give bonnet alignment.

In order to control any distortion of the bonnet when being closed by the handle an adjustable roller guide is bolted to its offside front corner. This engages with a striking plate on the cab side and guides the bonnet into its correct position.

A lock-catch guard is fitted to the underside of the bonnet to protect the lock catch when the bonnet is removed from the vehicle.

The radiator grille is detachable to expose the radiator and the front of the engine, and is supported at the bottom by two hooks on the body and secured at the top by two captive screws. These hooks are adjustable upwards and downwards. Also, the top fixing bracket is mounted on the front crossbrace and is adjustable sideways, which enables the grille to be centralised with the bonnet.

The underside of the front nearside canopy is fitted with a hinged flap that, when lowered by releasing the budget lock at the forward end, gives access to the signal bell cord and tangent switch with electrical connections, which are bolted in position to facilitate replacement. The Ranco valve and pipework associated within the heating system are also accessible through this flap.

All the canopy panels, however, can be taken down if necessary by removing the fixing screws and the screws attaching the grab handle. The vertical cover in the corner between cab and bulkhead can also be removed to access the pipework behind. The finisher panel at the bulkhead, which supports the destination slip plate (beside the canopy blind box), is removed in the same way.

The heat exchanger can be accessed by opening the front grille below the destination box using a budget key. It's hinged upwards and is retained in position by the strap provided at the left, which is placed on the hook above.

Ducting is mounted in the canopy to carry air to the upper passenger saloon, where outlets are arranged at five points at the front – one either side at the bottom-front window level and three at floor level, situated at each side and in the centre. The lower saloon outlet is positioned on the front saloon bulkhead at a point in line with the gangway approximately one foot above floor level.

A blind is provided for blanking off the heat exchanger and is controlled by a pull-cord from inside the driver's cab, above and to the nearside of the windscreen.

Earlier vehicles have a different type of installation in the lower saloon. The airflow from the canopy duct passes over a splitter, which directs a proportion down the vertical duct to a point just above the flywheel cowl, while the remainder passes through a special diffuser mounted just below roof level that's designed to deflect it to the sides of the vehicle. The upper saloon installation is identical on all vehicles. All production vehicles were later modified to standard.

The first 250 production vehicles had slot-type ventilators located above the upper saloon front windows. These incorporated a spring-loaded hinged flap controlled by a standard budget lock key, and were either open or shut.

Both upper and lower saloon floors consist of rectangular assemblies made from 20 SWG corrugated aluminium alloy sheet solid-riveted to a top aluminium alloy sheet of 18 SWG. These units are hollow-riveted to the main floor structure. It's important that the floor assemblies aren't drilled or cut under any circumstances, during accident, repair, rebuilding for other uses or at overhaul, as this may cause water leaks to occur, particularly through the upper saloon floor. A further aluminium sheet is, however, hollow-riveted to the undersurface of the lower saloon floor in order to prevent mud and dirt packing into the corrugations.

Water chutes are provided in the upper saloon floor coverings and drain ferrules in the lower saloon floor, thus permitting the drainage of water. These should be inspected and cleaned at regular intervals.

Both upper and lower saloon floors were originally covered with hard-wearing cork/rubber composition slats (or, later, Multislat matting) on the platform and gangways and plain matting, known as 'Treadmaster', elsewhere, which is fixed to the floor with a suitable adhesive. Some vehicles, including all of the RMLs later in the 1990s, had a hard-wearing material called 'Permatread' fitted under the seats.

In the lower saloon, a removable trap is built into the centre of the floor for the gearbox and a similarly removable cowl for the flywheel; both are secured by captive setscrews. A trap isn't fitted at the footstall over the rear axle, as the differential unit is fitted from underneath the vehicle. A removable trap secured by a budget lock is fitted on the offside to allow the fuel-tank pipes to be disconnected when removing the tank.

A portion of the gearbox trap rear support rail is made detachable and is secured by three setscrews, which enables this portion to be disconnected for the removal of the automatic gearbox AC signal generator (SSG).

Fresh-air ventilation is available by mechanically hand-wound quarter-drop windows controlled by the passengers. Twelve high-level windows of this type are fitted in the positions indicated below:

- Three nearside upper saloon in the second, third and fifth bays.
- Three offside upper saloon in the second, third and fourth bays.
- Two front upper saloon (in the first 250 production vehicles these were fixed windows).
- Two nearside lower saloon in the first and third bays.
- Two offside lower saloon in the first and third bays.

Spring catches are fitted externally at the bottom of the window slide-rail sections, which provides an additional drop to the window in order to facilitate cleaning the bar of the lower half when necessary. The spring catches must be in the 'up' position under normal operating conditions and are only lowered for cleaning purposes.

All window pans are attached to the body structure with Tucker Pop rivets with the exception of the pan in the lower saloon rear frame, which is secured instead with stainless steel screws (6 UNC) engaging with hardened steel insert bushes located in the body of the structure rails. The interior decorative plastic window finishers are held in position by the surrounding mouldings, with the edges adjoining the windows located in a groove extruded in the polished rim of the window pans. If it's necessary to replace a pan, the interior mouldings and plastic finishers have to be removed.

All windows are of toughened glass glazed into aluminium alloy pans, originally by means of a product known as 'Simplastic' glazing rubber. They're glazed from the inside of the saloon, as the window rubber is placed against an external lip on the pan. The only exceptions are the driver's cab offside quarter-light window, the upper deck rear emergency window and all destination boxes, which were glazed with 'Simpla' single-unit perimeter glazing rubber. All the drop windows, the lower saloon rear frame fixed window and the rear emergency window used 32oz toughened glass, while 26oz toughened glass was fitted to the lower half of the drop windows and the remaining fixed windows.

The upper saloon emergency window frame is made in polyester-reinforced fibreglass, designed as two separate sections that are bonded together during manufacture to form one unit.

The upper saloon has accommodation for 36 seated passengers, there being eight crosswise seats on the offside and ten on the nearside. Four seats on the nearside and four seats on the offside are fitted with floating stanchions. The lower saloon has seating accommodation for 28 passengers, having five crosswise seats on both nearside and offside and a four-passenger longitudinal seat over each wheel arch. Two crosswise seats on the nearside and two alternate seats on the offside are fitted with floating stanchions.

ABOVE Feed and dribble return connections are on the top of the fuel tank toward the rear and are accessible through a floor trap in the lower saloon.
(Mark Kehoe)

LEFT Many of the refurbished vehicles completed in the early part of the 21st century had the quarter-drop windows replaced by these hopper windows. There have been various suggested reasons why these were fitted, but they don't ventilate the vehicle as well as the original type.
(Andrew Morgan)

LEFT All RMLs had an additional emergency exit in place of one of the fixed lower-deck windows.
(Andrew Morgan)

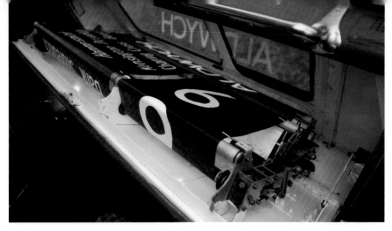

All the seat frames are of tubular steel construction, the gangway top rails, squab channels and stanchions being in polished stainless steel. At waist height the seat frames are secured by a stainless steel setscrew into a tapped boss. At seat level the seat frames are bolted to two mounting brackets attached to the body side. The seat legs are secured in place by setscrews that engage with floating nuts captive within the floor structure rail. Should they become damaged it's possible to replace these nuts by sliding them towards the large clearance hole situated at the centre beneath the foot of each chair leg and lifting the nuts out of the rail. Locating pegs are positioned within the floor rails to limit the travel of the nuts in an outward direction. When the seat legs are tightened down the floor covering is compressed to form a watertight connection.

Wooden blocks have been fitted within the roof structure to take the woodscrews that fix the top sockets for the stanchions. The seat stanchions are connected to the frames by an articulated cruciformed rubber encased inside a screwed stainless steel cap.

Upholstery

Moquette-covered seats were originally fitted to London Transport vehicles, in a pattern that was designed primarily for the Routemaster. The seat filling was originally a polyether foam but during 1960 this was changed to Vitafoam. The boards to the seat squabs and backs were originally moulded in fibreglass but were replaced from 1963 onwards by a steel bottom section and conventional $5/16$in (7.9mm) plywood back, as the fibreglass was found to break too easily.

The edges of the seats nearest the gangway were originally covered with red hide, while the seat backs were covered with grey-coloured 'leathercloth', which was known as Chinese Green and matched the internal panels around the windows.

Route destinations

London Transport manufactured their own individual destination blinds from screen-printed paper laid on to linen that could be mounted on rollers, so that the routes for a particular garage could all be included on one set. In total, seven individual blinds are required for a Routemaster, and when they were new this total was actually eight. Markings were printed on the rear of the blinds so that they could be correctly positioned in order for prospective passengers to read them.

Manufacture of the blinds was labour intensive and thus an expensive process, with individual letters being placed by hand prior to screen-printing. By the late 1980s production of the blinds was out-sourced, with stronger and more modern materials such as Tyvek being adopted, but once away from London Transport control they no longer used the familiar Johnston typeface. In the 1990s yellow on black luminescent type became standard to improve visibility for the partially or poor sighted. Unfortunately these seemed to look dirtier more quickly. Nowadays, with computer technology, improved typefaces and presentation have become available.

The front and rear route number, front route number, front and rear destination and front bulkhead route number indicators have conventional blind gears for the operation of the rollers. The nearside route indicator has an additional fixed jockey roller.

The offside route number, accessed through hinged panels in the conductor's locker, was discontinued during 1963 and removed when the vehicles were overhauled.

Paintwork and livery

Externally, Routemasters as they left the factory were hand-painted. London Transport spray-painted all vehicles during overhaul or intermediate repaints at Aldenham Works, using traditional oil-based paint. The spray process consisted of three coats applied while the previous one was still wet, finished with two coats of varnish followed by three hours in a drying oven.

Ancillary areas such as the relief band and wheels would have been hand-painted afterwards. The relief band has changed colour over the years, from a shade known as Chiswick cream, to flake grey and finally to white. The wheels were always painted in a colour called Indian red, which can be likened to a gloss red oxide, which is either a brown or a burgundy colour.

Repairs and repainting at the garages between visits to the works was undertaken with hand-applied brushing paints.

Over the last 20 years alternative paint types have been used, with two-pack acrylics and water-based paint now being standard.

The underside of the bodywork would have been finished with bitumen paint when new, but after overhauls this was painted silver as part of the spraying of underbody components. The subframes would have been painted in silver chassis paint, and were painted during overhaul away from the bodywork. All aluminium bodywork parts were treated in a pink primer undercoat. Any parts that were delivered to the garages to be fitted after accident damage were also pre-treated in this pink primer.

The battery compartment and the battery crate should always be painted with sulphuric acid-resistant black paint.

Internally, the ceiling panels were originally stove enamel-coated for durability, in a colour known as Sung yellow, which successfully masked nicotine stains. In later years a standard brush-applied paint was used. Subsequently white was used instead, and from the early 1990s a semi-gloss white was adopted for the RML refurbishment programme.

The lower panels below the windows were covered with maroon-coloured rexine. This was painted at overhaul with a special matt rexine paint. When new, Routemasters had the rexine applied to all areas including those around the platform and staircase. However, gloss burgundy paintwork was substituted later in the vehicle's life. Other miscellaneous one-off metal items, such as the flywheel cover and differential cover, were painted with gloss burgundy from new.

Dimensions and weight

The following table provides statistical details for the standard Routemaster variants. All vehicles are believed to be standard as per this list, unless otherwise rebuilt by or on behalf of new owners. (See Appendix 4 for an explanation of the code letters in the seating capacity column.)

Production vehicles						
Type	Length	Width	Height	Wheelbase	Weight	Seating capacity
RM	27ft 6½in	7ft 11½in	14ft 4½in	16ft 10in	7,366kg	H36/28R
RMC	27ft 6½in	7ft 11½in	14ft 4½in	16ft 10in	7,874kg	H32/25RD
RCL	29ft 10½in	7ft 11½in	14ft 5in	19ft 2in	8,255kg	H36/29RD
RML	29ft 10½in	7ft 11½in	14ft 5in	19ft 2in	7,874kg	H40/32R
RMA	27ft 6½in	7ft 11½in	14ft 4½in	16ft 10in	7,823kg	H32/24F
RMF	29ft 10½in	7ft 11½in	14ft 4½in	19ft 2in	7,849kg	H41/31F
FRM	31ft 3in	7ft 11½in	14ft 5in	16ft 10in	8,636kg	H41/31F
Post-production variants						
RM	27ft 6½in	7ft 11½in	13ft 9in	16ft 10in	7,021kg	O36/28R (open-top)
RMC	27ft 6½in	7ft 11½in	13ft 9in	16ft 10in	unknown	O32/25RD (open-top)
RMF	29ft 10½in	7ft 11½in	13ft 9in	19ft 2in	7,849kg	O41/31F (open-top)
RCL	29ft 10½in	7ft 11½in	14ft 5in	19ft 2in	unknown	varies (convertible or part open-top)
RME	31ft 8in	7ft 11½in	14ft 4½in	21ft 6in	8,210kg	H40/32F
ERM	31ft 8in	7ft 11½in	13ft 9in	21ft 6in	7,660kg	O44/32R (open-top)
DRM	29ft 10½in	7ft 11½in	14ft 5in	19ft 2in	7,951kg	H40/32RD

The prototypes were an exception to the standard production vehicles, although most of them were subsequently rebuilt to standard. The known exceptions to the rule are as follows:

RMC4 length is 27ft 3½in and weight 7,620kg.
RMF1254 seating capacity is H38/31F.
Cummins B-series-engined RMLs became 8,020kg.

Chapter Three

The owner's view

There are many types of owner, and over the 30 or so years that out-of-service Routemasters have been available they've been acquired for many different reasons by many different people. With a few exceptions, however, ownership is a great leveller, with everyone having one common interest: the Routemaster bus. Some owners say that owning a Routemaster is just like owning a very large car, but how easy is it to own a Routemaster, and what's involved?

OPPOSITE A row of different-coloured Routemasters at the 50th Anniversary Routemaster 50 rally in July 2004. *(Mark Kehoe)*

So who buys a Routemaster?

There are many reasons why people acquire a Routemaster, but here are some examples of typical Routemaster owners:

- The rally attendee who takes his Routemaster out most weekends in the summer.
- The owner who buys a Routemaster and then parks it up and never touches it again.
- The serious rally attendee who likes to enter judging and *concours d'élégance* competitions.
- The owner who likes to tinker with his Routemaster in the barn but rarely takes it out.
- A large group or syndicate formed to buy a Routemaster.
- A single individual owner.
- The chequebook preservationist who obtains professional help for any work undertaken on the vehicle
- The owner who carries out all the maintenance himself (or herself).
- A large collector who owns many vehicles.
- A mechanic or former professional mechanic.
- An ordinary working man (or woman) with no mechanical knowledge at all.
- ...Or someone who falls somewhere between all of the above!

Buying a Routemaster

There are various ways an individual or company can purchase a Routemaster. However, the main ways of purchasing – or selling – Routemasters are as follows:

- From a bus company.
- From a dealer, such as Ensign Bus.
- Direct from another private owner.
- From a company where it's previously been used as a non-psv/pcv.
- From a scrapyard.
- Via an Internet auction site or web-based forum.

These methods also apply if, for one reason or another, you decide that you no longer wish to keep your Routemaster and want to dispose of it. Unfortunately, for one reason or another, many Routemasters have been sold over the last few years, and as more have become surplus to the domestic market's needs numerous examples have been sold abroad.

It should be remembered that a number of features are unique to the design of the Routemaster and need to be checked when first viewing a vehicle with the intention of purchasing it. These include the following:

RIGHT The majority of vehicles that have been scrapped were cut up by PVS near Barnsley in South Yorkshire. Some RMs, such as these three, have had parts slowly removed for the last 17 years. *(Mark Priest)*

BELOW **BELOW** Behind the panels at floor level are, surprisingly, some steel brackets, which hold in place the cable conduits for the lighting circuits. After many years' service, however, they've usually started to corrode. *(Mark Kehoe)*

ABOVE One of the Routemaster's known areas of weakness has to be the B-frame. Older units corrode, which causes the flitch plates to push away from the main side members as rust forms between them. Above the B-frame, corrosion has been found to the box beam that has the connection from the Panhard rod. *(Andrew Morgan)*

- Check the condition of the B-frame – look for corrosion between the main side-frames and the flitch plates.
- Check the condition of the B-frame sandwich rubbers.
- Check for corrosion around the Panhard rod crossmember above the B-frame.
- Check the general condition of the brake system, including the accumulators, for leaks and knocking noises. Also check how quickly the flag rises and whether it will stay up, and if the warning lights go out after the engine has been started. Check if the flag stays up when the brakes are applied. This will give you an indication of the condition of the accumulators.
- Check for severe corrosion noticeable around the rivets on the beading and curved panels to the lower-deck ceiling – this could be a sign of problems and electrolytic action, as there are steel rivets, aluminium panels and some steel parts inside the bodywork.
- Beware of the wiring – it was originally aluminium, and due to age is breaking down on unrefurbished RMs. Although this is very difficult to spot, if electrical features don't work then there may be a problem.
- If you're buying a vehicle that requires rebuilding remember that items such as

LEFT The original cabling was aluminium and some has since been replaced by copper, but on the majority of RMs the older cabling could break down and the circuit fail, or, even worse, the insulation could fail. *(Brian Lewer)*

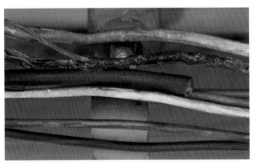

LEFT Melted cabling sends a shudder down the spine of any vehicle owner regarding what might happen next. *(Brian Lewer)*

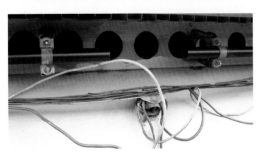

LEFT A new conduit has been fitted so that new cabling can be installed and the original bulb holders rewired. *(Brian Lewer)*

ABOVE A handful of RMLs were sold to PVS direct from the operating companies and all but one of these remain on-site.

(Tony Potter)

indicator brackets, AEC engines, differential casings and half-shafts are all difficult to locate.
■ Some other components can be refurbished, but the old removed unit should be retained so that a replacement part can be purchased on an exchange basis. These include accumulators, compressors and quill drives.

Running costs

Apart from major maintenance or restoration, the single largest cost of owning and using a Routemaster is fuel, especially at £6.40 per gallon (at early 2011 prices). The Routemaster was well known as the most fuel-efficient bus in the London fleet, often achieving seven to eight miles per gallon. In preservation condition, I always estimate that you can achieve 10mpg, and there have been times when vehicle owners have been known to achieve 17mpg on long runs, such as up and down the A1 between Yorkshire and London; but with no fuel gauge or milometer fitted – unless a tachograph has been installed – you're at best guessing the actual consumption,

with an accuracy of probably only plus or minus 10%.

The next big cost of owning a Routemaster, unless you own plenty of land, will be storage. In the United Kingdom this can be anything up to and above £25 per week, but the nearer you keep your bus to London then the dearer it will become.

A Routemaster is basically the ultimate 'big boys' toy', and maintenance costs won't be small. For example, original-style 6V Type 721 batteries will be over £100 each, and you need four per vehicle...

Road tax for preserved vehicles is currently nil cost for vehicles first registered before 1 January 1973 and not used for hire and reward. (Note: vehicles used for hire and reward would be class 6 pcv.) For vehicles used to carry passengers in revenue-earning service, the cost is £330 per annum unless a reduced pollution certificate (RPC) has been granted, when it's reduced to £165.

The United Kingdom MOT for a standard preserved Routemaster, *ie* one not used for hire and reward, is known as the class V test, and the current cost is £80.65.

Insurance costs can often be in the region of £100 to £250 per annum, depending on the declared value of the vehicle, for fully comprehensive cover. Several companies offer specialist insurance cover depending on the declared use.

You should always allow for some oil consumption – although with some engines this is low or minimal – and for general wear and tear, *eg* tyres and servicing. If you're unable to undertake the general servicing yourself you should allow a sum of money for this to be carried out on an annual basis by a competent mechanic or company.

Despite the best of care and intentions, general maintenance will always be necessary. Unless you've had a thorough rebuild undertaken, there will always be something that requires repairing or replacing. Remember, every Routemaster will be over 40 years old; I always think of Routemaster maintenance as being like owning a miniature Forth Bridge – by the time you get to one end, it will be time to start back at the other end again.

A surprising cost is when new destination blinds need to be purchased. A brand new set would easily cost in excess of £300 if they have to be manufactured, and would cost even more if they were a special one-off set. Original blinds auctioned on eBay have sold for up to £600 each, and at least seven blinds are required for a standard Routemaster.

The other important fact to remember is that Routemasters don't like being parked up; they need to be regularly driven, especially if they have hydraulic brakes, where lack of use can encourage condensation to form in important places such as within the brake accumulators.

If you're driving your Routemaster with more than eight passengers aboard, or are using it with profit in mind (for private hire and weddings, for example), then a tachograph must be fitted by law. Although there are some ways round this requirement, if you're in any doubt whatsoever you should seek advice. You may have insurance to cover you, but legally you could be breaking other regulations. Also, don't forget that once they're fitted tachographs need to be checked and recalibrated by an approved inspector.

Values

Basically, valuation of a Routemaster is quite difficult. Insurance companies will always want to know the value or replacement cost of your vehicle, but quite often owners inflate the value in an effort to recover the not inconsiderable costs spent on restoration and refurbishment. A sad fact of life is that you'll never recover the full costs spent on any historic or vintage vehicle, and anyone who thinks that they can will be sadly disappointed. Remember, owning a Routemaster is a hobby, not a money-making exercise.

Occasionally Routemasters can be purchased for scrap value or less, but these will be examples that have been severely cannibalised or are accident-damage victims, and will require a large amount of time, effort and money to be spent on them.

As a benchmark, the last known price for vehicles purchased from the PVS scrapyard near Barnsley was around £2,500 per shell, and these vehicles had been cannibalised and stripped for at least 17 years. You may pay anything between £5,000 and £10,000 for a vehicle that's run out of MOT, is in 'as withdrawn' condition, and has been off the road for some time; but the final price will depend on the overall condition of the vehicle and whether or not it's complete.

Even in these uncertain times, standard Routemasters (RM or RML types) can regularly be seen for sale at prices between £15,000 and £20,000, although for this price you'd expect to get a tidy example in reasonable condition.

For restored examples in good condition you'd expect to pay in the region of £20,000 to £25,000. An unrefurbished RM in original restored condition will have a market value at the upper end of this bracket.

Another factor that will increase the value of a Routemaster is whether or not it still has its original registration. A WLT--- registration will often sell for up to £1,500, whereas a plate with two numbers and three letters (for example VLT15) can easily be sold for £6,000. The original registration plate, after all, completes the vehicle.

Other vehicles known to be at or over the higher end of this price-range, depending upon their condition, would be the rarer RMC and RCL types.

Some vehicles have been known to sell for even higher prices, but these are generally examples that have been converted to new roles, including Routemasters rebuilt as mobile restaurants, or those fitted with new engines. The only other Routemasters that have been sold for unusually high prices have been one-off vehicles such as prototypes. In 2007 the fourth prototype, RMC4, was sold for – reputedly – in excess of £50,000.

Researching the history

For many owners, the history of a particular bus is very important. The detailed service history of the Routemaster has been researched and recorded by various individual enthusiasts and enthusiast groups. Naturally, with London having been its principal operational area the London Omnibus Traction Society, or LOTS as it's known (www.lots.org.uk), has discovered much of this. The data available will be able to confirm the date a vehicle was built, when and where it entered service, all of its various refurbishments, overhauls and intermediate repaints, transfers between various garages and its final withdrawal date. Its history will include particulars of any body changes and whether an AEC or Leyland engine was fitted, as well details of subsequent replacement by any other engine type, such as Cummins, Iveco or Scania.

The lives of Routemasters following their service with London Transport, London Country, British Airways or Northern General has generally been recorded by enthusiasts in a similar way where vehicles have gone on to undertake further passenger-carrying service. However, the subsequent history of a vehicle after its sale by a bus company can sometimes be a little uncertain, and the records for some become brief or non-existent, especially if they've been sold overseas.

Although there are a number of useful websites the information they provide is often incomplete, or omits the data that you may particularly want, and the very existence of some such sites is often brief. My own recommendation is that the Routemaster Association is the best place to start, since it holds records for *every* Routemaster, or is usually able to find somebody who can help.

Limits to authenticity

Since Routemasters first became available for sale in quantity the number of vehicles in original condition has decreased. For example, when London Transport was selling the first RMs in the mid-1980s they were in London Transport 'as withdrawn' condition. Inevitably, over the 40-plus years since they were manufactured individual vehicles have undergone hundreds of modifications at overhaul, numerous refurbishment programmes, or just been repaired in different ways at local garages, and the end result is that they're no longer in original condition.

Routemasters sold in more recent years have come from companies such as Stagecoach, where they've undergone various modifications to suit their new operations. Similarly, there have been numerous refurbishment programmes in London, some minor – such as the changing of rear lights or the fitment of fluorescent interior lighting – and some major, such as the refurbishment programme carried out to the majority of the remaining RML fleet between 1992 and 1994.

Therefore to recreate a Routemaster in original condition, a varying amount of work is required. But how far should you go to create a perfect example of a preserved Routemaster? Every Routemaster has its own story to tell, many having had lengthy histories and, often, numerous owners. So the choices of livery and condition if you're preserving a Routemaster can be many.

Also, it's worth bearing in mind that many modern or improved components have become available since Routemasters were manufactured, and it's up to the owner whether to fit a modern equivalent or not. Sometimes the original item is no longer available or can't be refurbished, and owners are left with little option but to find an alternative. Often a more modern equivalent can be fitted without any detrimental effect to the external appearance of the vehicle, though it might result in improved or reduced power consumption; an example is the fitment of modern alternators.

Below are a few things that should be considered when you're restoring a Routemaster and wondering whether you want to recreate its original condition:

- The lower deck panels were originally screwed but have often been riveted due to accident damage or refurbishment. Rivets may be easier to fit, but to be authentic screws should be reinstated. This is a classic example of a decision that needs to be based on how authentic you want your vehicle to be.
- Originally three 8V batteries were fitted and more recently four 6V batteries; due to the cost, many owners are fitting two 12V batteries instead. Of course, since they're hidden out of sight this doesn't affect the vehicle's external appearance either way.
- London Transport had exact design patterns and standards for all lettering applied to their publicity, buildings and vehicles etc, and after 1916 they used the Johnston font for all such purposes. Originally all vehicle lettering was applied as varnish-fix transfers, before being replaced by solvent-fix ones, and all were manufactured directly for London Transport. From the 1980s onwards vinyl transfers came into common use, but the standard of the lettering was very notably poorer, as other fonts were adopted when outside companies were employed. As vehicles have been preserved the standard of the lettering and transfers applied has similarly varied, with different fonts being used, often with incorrect spacing or even inaccurately positioned on the vehicle. Though these may look correct from a distance, close up they spoil what would otherwise be a very authentic-looking vehicle.
- Similarly, destination blinds can be quickly manufactured, but if they're badly produced they'll spoil the overall presentation of the vehicle.
- London Transport had their own advertising department, but with the adoption of vinyl adverts in the 1980s and then the adoption of advert frames, the size of advertisements has increased. This is particularly noticeable with the main side adverts, and the rear advert below the lower-deck window.
- Originally all of the seat cushions and backs had leather edges. Latterly London Transport omitted this as a cost-saving exercise (from the mid or late 1970s onwards). Not many preserved vehicles have been retrimmed with

leather, because although leather may look nice it's very expensive!
- Many owners have fitted chrome trim to the lights and the front wheels. Originally only special Routemasters that were used for trips abroad, or as 'Showbuses' in the early 1980s, had this. In addition, although chrome trim may look nice it takes time to keep clean and shiny and isn't actually correct.
- Most Routemasters were withdrawn with plastic Sparfax mirrors, but fitting the correct type will depend on the era that you're trying to represent. Also, bear in mind that the original mirrors are generally smaller (especially the nearside mirror, which was

ABOVE It's important to keep the battery compartment clean and treated with anti-sulphuric paint to stop any corrosion or electrolytic action occurring. *(Mark Kehoe)*

LEFT Fleet numbers make a vehicle look complete, but for an authentic appearance they have to be the correct font and size and in the correct position. The word 'ROUTEMASTER' over the fleet name continued on new vehicles until October 1964. *(Andrew Morgan)*

LEFT Registration numbers have changed in size, but to look correct the right font has to be used. Don't forget to get the spacing correct as well. *(Mark Kehoe)*

originally a small round type), and provide an inferior view for the driver. Consequently though you may want to fit original-type mirrors you might need to compromise by using larger ones.

■ Latterly a more modern type of windscreen was fitted that was originally supplied with a matt black frame. If the frame is simply painted black then from a distance you can't tell the difference, and will only be able to spot that they're different when you're close up. Also, these conversions to modern windscreens may mean that the upper and lower windscreens are now no longer able to open. Latterly the lower windscreens were modified with plates along the lower edges to stop the screen from opening.

■ Brake cooling grilles help make a Routemaster look as if it's in original condition, but only RMs up to RM1901 were fitted with them.

■ During the life of the Routemaster, headlamp panels became intermixed. Numerically, from the RCLs upwards the recess for the brake cooling panel fitted inboard and below the headlamps was omitted, and the bottom of the panel lined up with the bottom of the radiator grille. Routemasters were often seen looking lopsided, with one of each type. RMLs were often seen with RM ones, and vice versa.

■ Similarly, numerically from the RCLs upwards the radiator grille no longer incorporated the registration plate when they were originally delivered. However, when the RML fleet was fitted with new radiator grilles in the early 1990s they were, surprisingly, to the earlier style. Radiator grilles of the later type are now in short supply and to date only a few RMLs have been refitted with the original later style.

■ On RM1665 and from RM1680 onwards the radiator grille included the familiar triangle badge, and the roundel bonnet badge was no longer fitted.

■ RMs before RM1068 had the wearing strip on the drivers' cab door painted red from new.

■ Originally the used ticket bin on the bulkhead to the nearside of the platform was painted red, but from RM1064 it was painted black.

■ Similarly, the rear upstairs emergency exit originally had a transfer above it with the words 'EMERGENCY EXIT' in black, but this was latterly changed to white, before being changed to the modern green boxes with white lettering.

■ The offside route number blind box on the staircase panel always makes a Routemaster look original, but it was discontinued after RM1742.

■ Over 50 years of operation, livery and detail changes have occurred. The legal ownership of the fleet, for example: London Transport Executive briefly became London Regional Transport, which then became London Buses. London Buses then changed to the new operating companies upon privatisation of the London bus fleets. Similarly, as the vehicles were sold and joined the fleets of provincial operators a further set of details became applicable. Already, only some 25 years later, records of these liveries are already becoming sketchy, so getting the details correct can be more difficult.

RIGHT Original-style bonnet badge. *(Mark Kehoe)*

FAR RIGHT The traditional triangular badge on the radiator grille mimicked the AEC badge. *(Andrew Morgan)*

- All except the first 24 RMLs were delivered with their relief bands painted flake grey, but many preserved vehicles are now seen with these bands painted cream, though it's a livery that the majority of the red RMLs never carried when new.

- Similarly, none of these later RMLs carried the word ROUTEMASTER above the fleet number on gold. This was actually discontinued after RM2045.

- There are some easy fixes, for example when vehicles have been modified following the RML refurbishment programme. Front direction indicators can be changed back to 'ears', although supplies of the brackets are getting difficult to find or very expensive. Rear lights can be changed, and the fog light can be reinstated below the nearside headlight. The heater grille below the front blind box was panelled over and can usually be reinstated easily by removing the blanking plate, unless the vanes have been removed.

- Also, the ceilings can be repainted back to Sung yellow, although this does look a little odd if the Transmatic fluorescent lighting is still fitted. Originally these panels were stove enamelled, which is why the original paintwork lasted so long.

- Similarly, the RMLs had their seats trimmed with 'eyes down' pattern moquette but can be replaced with original-style moquette. The side walls were also trimmed in this moquette, and this can be replaced with rexine using a material very similar to the original. The front bulkhead to the lower and upper saloons originally had a 'pin-head' material that can best be described as 'table-tennis bat' material. To date nobody has sourced this and generally vehicles have had standard rexine applied instead.

- As part of the RML refurbishment programme, Transmatic fluorescent lights were fitted; these can be removed and tungsten bulbs refitted.

- Other Transmatic features included the Fibreshield roof dome to protect the original aluminium dome and be resistant to tree damage. These can be removed, but then your vehicle could become damaged more easily from overhanging trees, as pruning is rarely undertaken nowadays.

- All RML blind boxes latterly had fluorescent tubes fitted, but whether bulbs have been fitted on the few fully restored RML vehicles is difficult to see. Other refurbishments to various batches of RMs have included the

RIGHT Much debate takes place regarding the design of the original heater on the front bulkhead. RM5 has been restored with an early-style heater and the jury is out as to whether it's correct. The vertical 'chimney' has been removed in this view. *(Phil Swallow)*

RIGHT An early view of a Routemaster with the hole for the budget key that was used to open and close the tap that turned the early design of heating system on and off. *(London Transport)*

RIGHT The next design of heating had a horizontal slider, as refitted here to RM17. Also of note is the horizontal beading with burgundy-coloured insert that goes across the 'chimney'. *(Mark Kehoe)*

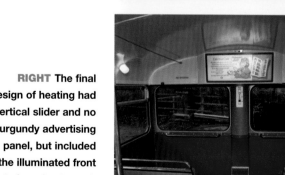

RIGHT The final design of heating had a vertical slider and no burgundy advertising panel, but included the illuminated front interior advert panel. *(Mark Kehoe)*

fitment of assorted types of fluorescent tubes in lieu of the tungsten bulbs. As with the RMLs, these can be removed and tungsten bulbs reinstated.

■ Similarly, it is easy to fit halogen H4 headlamp units and bulbs to provide better illumination, which is especially important when returning home from a rally or event in the dark. They aren't authentic, but it's very difficult to spot that they've been changed.

■ A modification late in the Routemaster's operational life was the fitment of single-piece wheels with 10.00 x 22.0 tyres (rather than the earlier 9.00 x 20.0 type). This is more noticeable than the change from cross-ply to radial tyres in earlier life, and looks instantly 21st century rather than 1960s.

■ Also, a common error is that the London Transport paint colour for wheels was known as Indian red; this was a cross between a glossy red oxide and maroon, but is often replicated today as a brown colour, which is totally incorrect.

■ With all the refurbishments and engine changes that took place in the late 1980s and 1990s, owners may wish to change the engine back to an AEC unit. However, there's a limited supply of these original units and one must question why you need to change a modern unit that's known to be reliable and for which parts can be obtained relatively easily.

■ Many owners would like to fit a higher-speed rear axle to improve the top speed of a Routemaster, especially when on long runs to events across the country. Some gains in fuel consumption are possible, and depending upon which unit is fitted top speed can be increased by as much as 28%; that doesn't sound much, but when some engines are governed down to 35mph (56.3kph) it could mean cruising at 45mph (72.4kph) instead. The standard AEC AV590 engine would cruise at 42mph (67.6kph) in some vehicles, and with a high-speed rear axle could cruise at 45–50mph (72.4–80.4kph) without pushing the engine at high revs all the time. The negative side of high-speed axles is that they're slow at accelerating from stationary and make town-driving more tedious. But whichever unit is fitted, you can't tell the difference from outside the vehicle.

■ Other features that were fitted during the lifetime of the Routemaster include the radio aerial on the roof dome, or in some cases domes. It's easy enough to remove this, but very few owners have. The radio equipment in the driver's cab will have been removed, but quite often the redundant cables will remain. Video cameras (although most were actually empty dummy units) and video advertising screens were fitted by some of the London operating companies late in their lives. These too can easily be removed, but reinstating them is more difficult where interior advert panels have been taken out, as these will have to be remanufactured.

■ There were several items that have never been reinstated. Originally Routemasters were built with rexine on the vertical panel under the bench seats, for example. The upper deck rear seat was originally built with an offside armrest up until RM1702, but, again, nobody has ever reinstated this feature.

■ Many Routemasters have been re-registered and have lost their original London registration numbers. Is a Routemaster correct with a non-London registration or one that's obviously been applied in the early 21st century rather than when it was built?

■ In many of the paragraphs above I've referred to vehicle numbers, but one shouldn't forget that after many overhauls at Aldenham Works the unique London Transport overhaul system meant that a high-numbered RM could receive a low-numbered body; so would it then be correct if it was restored to original condition? An extreme example is RM16, which in 1981 was outshopped from overhaul with body number B1888 from 1964 and fitted with a Leyland engine, so the owner of this RM has always chosen to preserve it in 1980s condition, as anything else would technically be incorrect. At the end of the day it's your vehicle and your choice.

■ And so the list could go on (and on!).

So how original do you make your vehicle? There have been many modifications during production, post-production, overhauls and refurbishment, and it's up to you whether any or all of them are reversed.

Restoration

For a long time now I've referred to the Routemaster as 'a glorified Meccano kit', and over the many years that I've been involved in the maintenance and restoration of them this has always proved to be the case. Any area of the vehicle can be dismantled, a replacement part substituted or the part overhauled and refitted, and the vehicle can then be reassembled with ease.

LEFT There are many different transfers all over the bodywork; some haven't been applied by the operators for many years, but they finish the presentation of a preserved vehicle. *(Mark Kehoe)*

BELOW RM13 was rescued after being cannibalised in a Barnsley scrapyard for 12 years. A few months after restoration commenced this was what the owner was faced with: there was a lot more missing than had appeared at first inspection. *(Andrew Morgan)*

The high quality of build of the Routemaster has been further acknowledged in probably the strangest place, namely in the scrapyard, where dismantling a Routemaster took longer than other vehicles of similar age. With little or no use of steel or timber in their bodywork, scrapping involved more dismantling by cutting up than was normally required, and corrosion was virtually non-existent. The preservationist restoring a 50-year-old Routemaster will encounter these same characteristics.

As further proof of this, whilst taking detailed photographs for this publication we witnessed 50-year-old components being removed, taken apart, serviced or rebuilt and reassembled for immediate reuse; so though this phenomenon may be unheard of for other vehicles it's totally normal for this one.

The Routemaster wasn't designed in the throwaway society that is 21st century Britain, but in a time when components were built to last and could be repaired. London Transport had systems in place whereby parts were removed and returned to either Chiswick or Aldenham Works for assessment and repair or refurbishment where possible. Although the world has changed, and replacement parts are nowadays fitted to modern buses on a daily basis, the era of parts being refurbished in quantity as carried out by London Transport has long gone. However, it's highly unlikely that today's buses will still be able to be dismantled, refurbished and reassembled by relatively low-skilled operatives when they're 50 years old.

Another feature of life that's changed over the last 50 years is that the records retained by

FAR LEFT Although the Routemaster has an aluminium body, there are odd pieces of wood in the framework which are usually there so that various items can be screwed together. Here the platform grab-rail over the ticket box is screwed into a wooden block located in the vertical framework.
(Brian Lewer)

ABOVE MIDDLE At the rear, the original-style tail lights are located in a special timber pattress. With the exterior panels removed these can be easily replaced.
(Mark Kehoe)

ABOVE RIGHT The seat-frame stanchions and handrails have timber blocks mounted in the ceiling for the top fixings.
(Mark Kehoe)

LEFT After years of hard service this is what vehicles generally look like once they've been stripped of seats, lighting systems and soft trim. For RMLs, the restoration commences here.
(Brian Lewer)

ABOVE Clayton heating systems are usually full of debris and working very inefficiently. Under the soft trim the remnants of the old side-wall coverings are still showing. The flooring still has Permatread laid over the aluminium floor. If this is to be removed, many hours of work lie ahead. *(Brian Lewer)*

BELOW Stripped to bare aluminium, and with various components unbolted for separate restoration, including the windscreen and emergency exit window, this is an unusual view of an RM cab. *(Mark Kehoe)*

BELOW RIGHT With the control box cover removed and the rear bulkhead stripped to bare aluminium, the CP13 control panel is visible. The hook is for holding down the night blind across the window between the driver's cab and passenger saloon. The brass plaque reveals that this is RM254. *(Mark Kehoe)*

bus companies are no longer kept to the same standards. This may be due to the way that buses are no longer operated by a large public sector body, such as London Transport, and to the fact that following the 1980s and 1990s privatisation process the companies are now much smaller, and cost is often the name of the game, with accountants holding the purse strings.

Up until the end of the 1980s London Transport religiously kept thorough records of every bus in their ownership. As well as the statutory records, they recorded every key unit number fitted to the vehicle, any changes to these, every repaint, every overhaul and any maintenance carried out on the vehicles themselves or the units fitted to them. They also had fastidious records of the mechanical and electrical units together with all the maintenance and overhaul procedures for them. All of this work was, of course, carried out in-house at London Transport's various premises. However, when these facilities closed this all ceased, and keeping records of the units fitted and any subsequent changes also ceased.

As described in Chapter 1, over the next 15 years engines were changed for more modern types and numerous refurbishments were carried out by many different companies, but very few records of these changes were kept by London Transport or their descendant companies. Now, with the majority of the

vehicles and companies in private hands, it's become apparent that little or no information was recorded or archived regarding new mechanical units, refurbishments or conversions. Whilst researching this book this problem has been encountered time and time again. It's therefore quite difficult for new owners to locate information for particular vehicles, especially as, for example, a Scania engine as operated by one company may have been fitted by a different company than the same type of Scania engine fitted to a different but essentially similar vehicle.

What's happened over the subsequent years is that various owners or operators have contacted companies such as Cummins and Scania and had various degrees of success in obtaining information about their vehicles. Typically the manufacturers can identify the actual engine from its unit or engine number. There have been many instances where Scania, for example, has been able to provide owners with a printout showing the actual build specification for the engine fitted to their own vehicle. Similarly, when provided with a serial number (or ESN) Cummins have been able to reveal when and where an engine was built, as well as confirming the type of engine fitted, although most owners will probably already know this. Information is also usually available through various websites, web-based forums and the Routemaster Association.

LEFT New kick plates complete the presentation to this nearly finished vehicle. Note the late-style Treadmaster flooring on the platform with narrow slats.
(Mark Kehoe)

LEFT Restoration of the interior can include the replacement of rexine on the side walls and repainting of ceilings, as well as replacement of the Treadmaster floor coverings. One of the hardest jobs is removing the old material and cleaning up the aluminium.
(Andrew Morgan)

LEFT With the new Treadmaster TM4 mat laid – and in this case 3in-wide gangway slats as well – the new flooring can be sealed using the recommended sealant or a varnish. The holes for the seat-frame fixings have to be cut out and the seats refitted. *(Andrew Morgan)*

LEFT The 3in-wide gangway slats have to be laid so that they're straight, with the correct gap between them. Originally, individual slats were supplied, but nowadays careful cutting is required, for example around the differential housing.
(Andrew Morgan)

RIGHT Listing of
suppliers as produced
by the Routemaster
Association.
(Andrew Morgan)

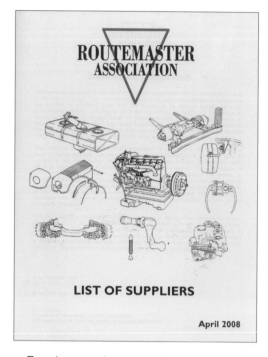

BELOW Corrosion
has been found in
the panhard rod
crossmember that
fits at the rear of
the B-frame. A
reproduction unit is
seen here beside a
corroded example.
(Andrew Morgan)

The Routemaster industry

Not surprisingly, the most common initial source of information for the Routemaster is the Internet. One of the most often used forums is the ROOF website at www.rmoof.co.uk.

If you carry out a search on the Internet through any search engine, numerous Routemaster references can be found, but the Routemaster Association website (www.routemaster.co.uk) is invariably one of the highest-placed. The Routemaster Association aims to provide not only one of the best websites but also to be a good starting point for locating other organisations or companies connected with Routemasters in some way. If you still can't find what you're looking for, then there's usually someone on this website who can be contacted who'll know how to help or can provide the answer that you require.

One further source of historical information is the London Transport Museum. However, you'll need to book an appointment if you want to view their archives or visit the Acton Depot.

A 'cottage industry' has grown up of people and small companies that can supply individual parts or trim items for Routemasters. However, the original large industry suppliers also generally remain in existence, although their output of Routemaster-related items has reduced dramatically, and with demand having diminished the items that are still available may no longer be readily obtainable 'off the shelf'. Imperial Engineering in Hertfordshire and Queensbridge PSV in West Yorkshire are two examples. Both have an immense amount of Routemaster-related knowledge in their areas of expertise, as they've been involved with the Routemaster vehicle for many years.

If it's a spare part from a scrap vehicle that you need, then the PVS scrapyard near Barnsley in South Yorkshire is still home to several Routemasters, some of which – as we have seen – have been undergoing long-term cannibalisation for up to 17 years.

Now, over five years since the large-scale operation of Routemasters ceased, this mix of major industrial suppliers, cottage industry providers and Internet sources is what will help you to keep your Routemaster on the road. A list of useful contacts is included in Appendix 6.

Experience to date suggests that when you contact the correct department of the relevant company you can obtain all the assistance you may require. Operation and maintenance manuals are available for all engine types, even though production ceased many years ago. The Cummins B-series engine, for example, is a Euro II unit, whereas Cummins is at the time of writing building the Euro V version.

For the gearbox, the original Wilson unit is still supported by specialist refurbishment companies, whilst the two variants of the modern Allison unit are supported by the manufacturer's UK agent. As with the engines, operation and maintenance manuals are available for all types of gearbox.

How to enter the driver's cab

Grab both handles, place left foot in the step...

...place right foot in the doorway; and...

...climb into the cab with left foot leading. *(Mark Kehoe)*

Driving and handling

A Routemaster is generally easy to drive. It has two-pedal control, *ie* accelerator and brake, being essentially an automatic vehicle with no clutch or operating pedal.

With an excellent view from the cab, you're high up and above other drivers. Remember, your vehicle is larger than most other vehicles on the road, and as soon as you understand its size your confidence will grow in terms of placing it where you want it to be. Also, other drivers of large vehicles will give you respect and allow you the space that you need. A novice Routemaster driver will always need to be wary of the nearside and where it is in relation to the kerb or parked vehicles.

With power-assisted steering and an automatic gearbox, driving a Routemaster isn't difficult. However, some owners will opt to adapt the gearbox to remove the automatic option, so that it's controlled manually, although there are still only two pedals. Although several types of engine and two main types of gearbox are fitted,

once under way the driving of vehicles equipped with any of these variants is very similar.

Nevertheless, it's often noted that no two Routemasters are the same to drive. This can be due to the set-up of the steering and different suspension components, as well as the general age or wear of the units. Some vehicles may have heavy steering whereas others may be finger-light.

The driver's cab is, shall we say, basic but functional, with the minimum of instruments and switches. These are in two places: to the right-hand side and high up on the left above the driver's shoulder. Don't forget that this is a bus, so the other equipment in the cab enables the driver to carry out his duties. There are places to put his time-card, with a light to read it in the dark, plus a periscope to view the destination blind and a winding handle to alter it at the end of the route.

To assist entering and exiting the cab there are handles plus a step for the left foot. The cab is then accessed via a sliding door, which means that it doesn't matter how close to the

ABOVE Over two years of preparation went into readying RM16 for a full external repaint.
(Andrew Morgan)

RIGHT After repaint into mid-1980s livery and the application of transfers and adverts, the finished result makes all the effort worthwhile.
(Mark Kehoe)

next vehicle you park (so long as you leave yourself room to climb out!). The door has a sliding window, primarily for signalling to fellow motorists but also for ventilation. The emergency window to the left likewise slides at the front for ventilation, and can also be used by the driver to talk to other members of staff without them having to stand in the road beside the vehicle. The windscreen originally opened for further ventilation by winding handles for both sections, but latterly these were fixed in the closed position. Two vents are positioned below the facia board, one for the heater and the other for fresh air. However, with the door and all these windows and openings, as well as the gaps in the floor around the handbrake and steering column, the driver's cab can be drafty and difficult to keep warm on very cold days. If you're travelling at speed in the winter, be prepared to wrap up warm.

Behind the driver is a window that looks into the passenger saloon. Originally this was a fixed piece of glass, but many owners have fitted an opening window so that passengers or the conductor can communicate with the driver.

Rear-view mirrors are fitted to the corners of the vehicle, and generally the later the mirror type the larger the mirror and the better the rearward vision. Remember that an RCL, RMF or RML has a wheelbase 2ft 6in (0.76m) longer than an RM, RMA or RMC. It can take a few moments to adjust yourself to this additional length.

The driver's seat can be adjusted vertically and horizontally by the operation of two winding handles located on the front, but adjustment shouldn't take place while the seat is occupied. When starting the vehicle, don't attempt to drive off until the red warning 'STOP' flag has lifted and the white light has gone out. These signals indicate that the gearbox and brake systems are working satisfactorily.

The inevitable paperwork

There are some key items of paperwork that apply to every Routemaster owner, though they'll vary in type, complexity and cost depending on the intended use of the vehicle. They are as follows:

- V5 registration document.
- Road tax.
- Insurance.
- MoT/PSV as applicable.
- Relevant driving licence for the driver.
- Operator's licence if applicable.
- Tachograph records if required.

The likely costs associated with these items are shown in the running costs section above.

BELOW Finally, this former BEA Routemaster that became an RMA used as a training vehicle with no staircase was acquired from a scrapyard and rebuilt; however, it was rebuilt a full bay longer by separating the body and bolting it back together. Again, a true testament to the Routemaster's jig-built construction and interchangeability of parts. *(Mark Kehoe)*

Chapter Four

The mechanic's view

━━(●)━━━━━━━━━━━

The Routemaster was a design that was ahead of its time, so that although in the 21st century gearboxes may have become more advanced and hydraulic brakes may have gone out of favour, the technology used at the time can still be understood, and it's consequently relatively easy to maintain Routemasters and keep them operational.

London Transport produced a maintenance bulletin in 1961, and other manuals are available that give more detailed technical information, but hopefully this chapter will give readers an insight into the daily and annual care and general maintenance requirements of a Routemaster.

OPPOSITE **Checking the engine oil on an AEC-engined Routemaster. Note the ease of access to the engine bay.** (Mark Kehoe)

Recommended lubricants and fluids

As described further on, lubricants should be checked at regular intervals and changed as required. Below is a list of the recommended lubricants for the various mechanical installations. For the older AEC and Leyland engines, Morris Lubricants have kindly provided details of their current equivalent products:

Installation	Litres	Lubricant
AEC/Leyland engine	approx 21.6	Morris Lubricants Golden Film SAE 30.
Scania engine	approx 20	SAE 15W-40 engine oil.
Cummins C-series engine	approx 22.4	SAE 15W-40 engine oil.
Iveco 836/1 engine	approx 20	Duplex CDX 15W/40.
Cummins B-series engine	approx 16.4	Ring Free MXC 15W/40.
Fuel pump (cam box and governor)		Morris Lubricants Golden Film SAE 10W to AEC and Leyland engines.*
Fluid flywheel	approx 14.8	Morris Lubricants Golden Film SAE 30.
D182-type gearbox (GB32)	approx 11.4	Morris Lubricants Multitrans BC.
Allison MT643 gearbox	approx 14	Dexron III, or the newer Dexron VI oil, or a TES295 specification oil such as Castrol TranSynd or BP Autran Syn 295.
Allison T270 gearbox	approx 25	BP Castrol ATF TQ DIII or BP Castrol Transmax DEX-III Multivehicle.
Rear axle/differential	approx 4.3	Morris Lubricants Golden Film AG90 or Lodexol Ultra Drive 80W/90.
Steering column/box	approx 3.4	Morris Lubricants Golden Film AG140.
Hydraulic brakes and power steering	approx 3.4	Morris Lubricants Liquimatic No 2.
Compressor	approx 0.4	Morris Lubricants Golden Film SAE 10W.
Thrust buttons		Morris Lubricants Golden Film AG90, (and lithium grease to the grease nipple points above).
Unloader valve (for winter operation)		Silicone-based grease.
Hubs		Lithium grease, such as Morris Lubricants 42EP lithium multipurpose grease.
Brake adjusters		
Propeller Shafts		

* The DPA fuel pump does not have a separate oil system.

For general greasing, the universal lithium-based grease should be used. (Do not apply handfuls of grease inside the hubs as this will lead to breakdown of the grease in the future; only a limited amount should be applied.)

There are numerous greasing points around the Routemaster that utilise the standard ³⁄₈in BSF hook-on nipples. The hydraulic (push-on) 45° angle type are for oil (and not grease) – for example, two ³⁄₈in BSF examples can be found on the steering relay oil baths to the rear of the front axle. An oil such as Morris Lubricants Golden Film SAE 30 should be pumped into these baths. An ideal method for carrying out this operation, if you don't have a pump, is to use an old grease gun. There are smaller examples on the saloon window winder bars and on the driver's cab windscreens, and lithium grease should be used in these.

The total amount for the coolant system for the original AEC and Leyland-engined examples is approximately 36.4 and 40.9 litres respectively. Similarly, the total amount required for the Scania engine's coolant system is around 45.0 to 50.0 litres, and the Cummins C-series engine approximately 50.0 litres. Figures for some of the other engines aren't known, but similar quantities would be expected.

The quantity of antifreeze to be included within the coolant should never be less than 25%, and never more than 50%, but the exact percentage will vary depending on the likely temperatures expected and the protection required.

For more modern engines such as the Cummins C-series a coolant additive is required, for which further details are given in the 'Maintenance' section below.

Safety first!

No apologies for stating the obvious – these are *large* vehicles. Rule number one, therefore, is *don't take risks.*

By definition, a large vehicle has large and heavy components that can be difficult and awkward to handle and should always be treated with appropriate care.

Numerous specialist tools and rigs were used by the original maintenance organisations, but these are very rarely seen or used today as they're no longer available. If in doubt, always seek professional help, advice or assistance before starting any work that you're not familiar with.

A few sensible reminders:

- Always apply the handbrake and chock the wheels.
- Stand the vehicle on firm and level ground.
- Use appropriate jacks, stands and lifting equipment.
- Use the correct jacking points or body support points. Each side-member carries jacking pads immediately fore and aft of the rear axle mounting position.
- If jacking a vehicle, always use a suitable secondary support if you're working underneath it.
- Beware of systems under pressure – for example, coolants, hydraulic fluid and compressed air.
- Always wear protective clothing where appropriate.
- Beware of dust from brake linings. Brake linings made of asbestos can still be found fitted to some vehicles.

Tools and working facilities

As noted above, various specialist tools were designed by AEC and London Transport for use by their original maintenance organisations. It's unlikely that many of these will be available today, so tools will have to be borrowed or manufactured to suit your needs. Details of some of these are available from enthusiasts and support organisations, but generally such tools aren't available to the average owner, so if a particular tool is required

it may be worth contacting the Routemaster Association or one of the Routemaster web-based forums to request advice and assistance.

The original Routemaster was manufactured in the days when everything was in imperial dimensions, with Whitworth products being common across the mechanical components and UNC/UNF for the bodywork. With the replacement of the AEC engines and gearboxes by modern engines and transmissions metric dimensions came into use, and vehicles can therefore be found with both imperial and metric fittings.

When you speak to mechanics, you'll find that they all have their own favourite tools. Examples include:

- A complete AF and metric socket set.
- A $^3/_8$in Whitworth spanner.
- A 19mm spanner (for injector pipes).
- A stubby screwdriver.
- A very long-shafted screwdriver.
- Two 1½in ring spanners (for the Panhard rod).
- An 8mm socket for undoing the driver's cab fittings.

Daily checks

It's advisable to get into the habit of checking the following items on a daily basis:

BELOW The dipstick tube on AEC and Leyland engines is located beside the engine oil filler on the nearside corner of the engine bay.
(Mark Kehoe)

RIGHT Lift the brass cap and fully insert the dipstick... *(Mark Kehoe)*

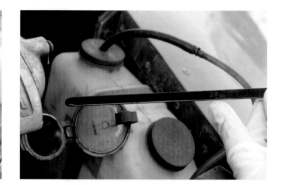

FAR RIGHT Lift out the dipstick and check to the relevant mark (as indicated). *(Mark Kehoe)*

OPPOSITE To carry out any maintenance, access underneath your Routemaster is a must, but few owners have the benefit of vehicle lifts. *(Andrew Morgan)*

RIGHT Clean windscreen. *(Andrew Morgan)*

BELOW Check mirrors. *(Mark Kehoe)*

- Water levels – coolant to the header tank.
- Engine oil – using the dipstick.
- Fuel level – manually check the fuel tank.
- Screen wash level (if fitted).

Don't forget to replace the relevant caps securely afterwards, especially the engine oil, otherwise fuming is likely to occur.

In addition, as part of your normal routine before setting off on the road you should always check the following:

- That the windscreen is clean.
- The condition of the windscreen wiper.
- That the headlamps, sidelight, rear lights, brake lights and all indicators are in working order.
- The adjustment and cleanliness of the mirrors.
- The operation of the horn.
- The condition of the tyres.
- The operation of the doors (where fitted).

Upon starting the engine, always wait until both warning lights have gone out and the flag has gone up before you drive off.

Annual servicing

Standard annual checks and inspections should be undertaken as good practice, with all major units being checked, whether the vehicle is used in passenger service or not. In London Transport days there was a standard four-week rota, with more work being required at weeks 8, 16 etc, and 'basic rota' being undertaken at weeks 4, 12, 20 etc. The 12th rota in the series was at week number 48, which was the annual inspection and preparation prior to the vehicle's annual test; for this rota the vehicle was usually off the road for at least two weeks whilst the work

Removing the nearside wing

(all Mark Kehoe):

1 Unscrew the radiator grille.

2 Remove the radiator grille.

3 Unbolt the front cross-brace.

4 Remove the front cross-brace.

5 Remove the electrical plug.

6 Unbolt the mounting bolt.

7 Remove the mounting bolt.

8 Remove the cover plate and unbolt the two lower bolts.

9 With the aid of a helper, lift the complete wing up...

10 ...and clear of the vehicle.

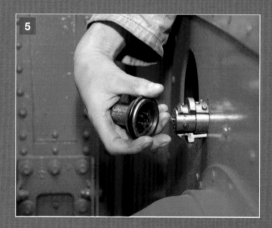

was completed. Often units would be changed whether they needed it or not.

The London Transport inspection procedure listed the following works checks for the 'Basic Inspections' at weeks 4, 12, 20 etc; this routine is still a good basis on which to plan for the inspection of each item and the servicing work that should be undertaken:

- Check engine and mountings; idling speed, and adjust if necessary; throttle gear; oil leaks generally; radiator tie rods; side covers for oil and water leaks; water system including heating and cooling radiators for leaks and overflow; condition of hoses.
- A, B and lower frames – check for cracks, check unit-mounting bolts; lubricate frame points (A-frame, B-frame and lower frame), silent bloc mounting and buffers.
- Transmission – check fluid flywheel for leaks and top up if necessary; differential for play; cardan coupling bolts and shield, lubricate coupling; all glands for leakage; check differential and gearbox levels and top up if necessary.

Checking the gearbox oil

(all Mark Kehoe)

1. The gearbox trap is in the centre of the lower saloon.
2. Lift the small cover by turning the lock with a budget key and slide out to reveal the dipstick underneath.
3. Lift the dipstick to check the oil; it should be at the lower mark as indicated.

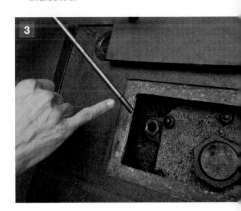

RIGHT The MoT examiner will check the security of the fuel tank cap and the seal inside it. *(Mark Kehoe)*

RIGHT Regularly check wheel nuts; use a torque wrench set to 400–450lb/ft, and if using a wheel-nut gun never let it hammer the nut. Some companies use wheel-nut markers or indicators as standard practice. *(Mark Kehoe)*

RIGHT The front brake adjuster; but don't forget that the offside adjuster should be turned clockwise and the nearside one anticlockwise. *(Mark Kehoe)*

- Change other filters as fitted (*eg* to Allison gearbox).
- Air pressure system – check manual for compressor bolts, pulleys, oil level.
- Fuel system – check the fuel shut-off cock, fuel pump for leakage, fuel tank for security and leakage; check the complete fuel system for leakage; check the fuel pump cam box and governor casing and top up if required; check all hoses and pipes for condition.
- Suspension system – check road springs for fracture and/or air springs for operation and security, clamp bolts for tightness, levelling valve for leaks, shock absorbers for leaks, security and fractures.
- Road wheels – check all wheel nuts for tightness.
- Steering gear – check movement to full lock, linkage and ball joints; lubricate, clean and re-grease bright steering parts; ensure drag link is correctly set; check steering box and power steering for leakage and operation, components for tightness and defects; check oil levels (see page 106 for the correct oil to be used in power-steering).
- Brakes – check handbrake operation and performance; brake liners for thickness (through observation hole) and adjust; brake valve cylinders and pipes for leaks and chafing; brake fluid level (check brake tank/reservoir sight glass) and top up if necessary; check system as defined in technical instruction/manual.
- Miscellaneous mechanical checks – the exhaust system, all belt drives and couplings, pedal pads for wear.
- Electrical – check lamps (including fluorescent tubes where fitted) and change those found to be defective; check bell pushes, bell and buzzer for operation, windscreen wiper, heater fan motor, horn, trafficators, engine starter switch, stop light return spring, alternator belt tension, speedometer transmitter and head; check/top up batteries and ensure tight connections; check engine stop switch; ensure that speed sensitive generator and connections are secure; check security of all units and ancillaries, *ie* alternator belts, compressor belts, all mountings etc.

Accessing the batteries

(all Mark Kehoe):

1 Unscrew the two large-diameter screws...

2 let the panel fall forwards...

3 ...and lift off the two locating lugs.

4 Rotate the two fasteners 90°...

5 ...to release the fibreglass side shield.

6 Slide it to one side and lift out...

7 ...to reveal the batteries.

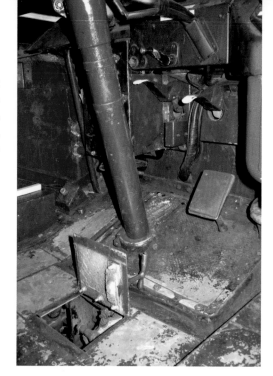

- Driver's cab – check seat, handbrake lever clip, windscreen operating gear, emergency window, sliding door, pad saw and fasteners, fire extinguisher, heater blind and cord.
- Bodywork external – check driver's mirrors, bonnet top and side, wing fixings, lifeguards, body fixing bolts, proud screws and rivets in panels and strap plates etc; EP and

electrically-operated doors for operation; and lubricate parts where necessary.
- Internal bodywork – check fixed and drop lights, floor treads and slats, floor traps, seats/seat frames (for condition and security), handrails, stanchions, platform, staircase, emergency doors and windows, blinds and boxes, also winding gear, proud screws and rivets in panels etc; lubricate parts where necessary.
- Vehicle cleaning – external wash and internal, vacuum clean cushions, clean paintwork (damp swab if necessary), including lamp bulbs, staircase stringer band and canopy etc; wipe down polished metal parts with white spirit.

Other work that should form a good basis as part of an annual major service routine, or annual MoT preparation, would be as follows:

- Change engine oil and oil filter (if fitted).
- Check and adjust tappets and oil feed to rockers. Remove radiator overflow pipe and ensure free water flow.
- Change/clean fuel filter element.
- Check steering for tracking and rectify if necessary. Top up steering box. Check for lift and rock.
- Check all lubricants and grease all points.
- Lubricate wheel hubs.
- Check pneumatic and hydraulic system as per manual.
- Change differential oil.
- Remove and refit starter. Lubricate alternator when necessary. Remove, clean and refit batteries. Paint battery crate when necessary. Clean saloon and destination lamps.
- Focus head and fog lamps. Check leads and connections and test for earth leakage. Check regulator. Check throttle control switch.
- Paint wings, lifeguards, dress shields, wheels and staircase as necessary. Touch up paintwork where necessary. Replace transfers and statutory notices when necessary.
- Full internal clean (as per 'Vehicle cleaning' paragraph above).
- Steam-clean the underside.

The 'Basic Inspection' tasks listed above are still valid today, but with the reduced mileage of preserved vehicles the additional tasks may not all be necessary, with the exception that engine oil should always be changed annually, whatever the mileage, as it deteriorates with time as much as use. The only other point to note specifically is that the differential oil should be changed every two years.

Maintenance

One of the best pieces of advice I can offer, especially if you've just purchased your vehicle, is to arrange for a knowledgeable mechanic or competent owner to look at the general condition of your Routemaster. This way you'll learn a great deal about your bus.

Below are the key things to look out for whilst undertaking maintenance on a Routemaster, starting with the engine types, including the modern varieties fitted over the last 20 years:

AEC AV590 engine

Change the oil filter at the same interval as the engine oil.

Check that the fan behind the radiator is running correctly relative to the radiator. If the blades become bent or damaged then catastrophic damage may result, including the radiator becoming damaged with the resultant loss of coolant.

Check for oil leaks; these could be a sign of later problems.

Leyland 0600 engine

Head gaskets! Any mechanic will tell you that replacing these this isn't a quick job. Also, beware of broken pipes to the injectors, which are located in the head itself: if the injector pipes break inside the rocker cover the leaking fuel can fill the engine with diesel, causing it to run away.

The Leyland engine installation was designed to be interchangeable with the AEC unit. There's a list of components that need to be changed or swapped over, but otherwise it's a straightforward job to switch these engines.

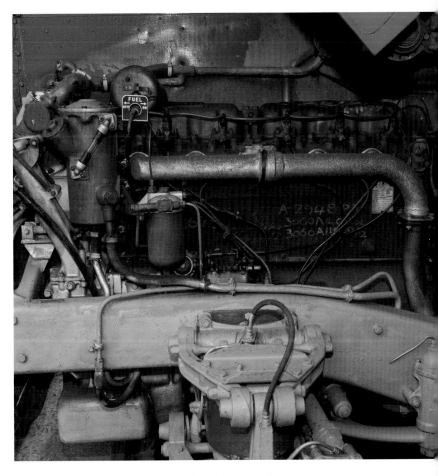

ABOVE The original AEC AV590 engine. *(Mark Kehoe)*

BELOW The Leyland 0.600 engine is fully interchangeable with the AEC engines. *(Mark Kehoe)*

ABOVE The Iveco 836/1 engine uses a new rear crossmember and a modified front crossmember.
(Andrew Morgan)

BELOW The Cummins C-series engine uses new front and rear crossmembers.
(Mark Kehoe)

Iveco 836/1 engine

It's recommended that valve clearances are regularly checked.

The standard AEC fluid flywheel is used, but the engine half is unique to the Iveco unit, together with the spigot bearing on the runner shaft.

The Kleenoil bypass filter must be changed at the same interval as the engine oil. Upon refilling with oil, start the engine and recheck after allowing the oil to fill both filter elements.

Corrosion inhibitor is recommended in the cooling system to prevent pitting and damage to the cylinder liners. There's a water filter cartridge fitted that must be regularly replaced, or changed whenever the cooling system has been drained.

Check the condition of the air intake filter and change as required, depending upon which unit is fitted. Some vehicles were fitted with a depression indicator between the filter and inlet manifold which shows the filter condition. Note: check the security of the air intake canister fittings, as they've been known to work loose and to catch fire, with dire consequences.

As part of major servicing, fuel injectors should be removed for cleaning and break-pressure testing, the fuel filter element should be changed, the gauze element and sediment bowl should be cleaned, the condition and tension of the drive belts should always be checked, and the idling speed should be checked to ensure economy and smooth running.

Cummins C-series engine

Cummins recommend that the oil levels, coolant level and fuel water trap are inspected daily or when refuelling. Preventative maintenance can be assisted by checking for general leaks, loose or damaged parts, worn or damaged belts and any changes in engine appearance.

The coolant system must contain the correct coolant additive to provide the best chemical protection, and must be to the correct concentration – a DCA4 coolant test kit is recommended by Cummins. The coolant filter assembly is part number WF9006 and the filter itself (or DCA4 corrosion resistor cartridge) is part number WF0207300 (DCA stands for 'diesel coolant additive').

Note: the eight-digit engine serial number (see the plate on the front of the engine above the radiator fan, just behind the water filler) will help Cummins service centres to correctly identify the engine and the relevant parts, filters and additives required for it.

At the end of every 12 months, 1,000 hours or 20,000 miles, Cummins recommend that the valve lash clearance is adjusted, and the air cleaner, intake system, antifreeze, fan hub, belt tensioner bearing and belt tensions are inspected. The lubricating oil, oil filter, coolant filter and fuel filter should also be changed at this time.

Scania DS9 engine

As with the Cummins engine, Scania recommend that the oil level, coolant level and air-cleaner vacuum sensor, as well the drive belts, are checked on a daily basis.

At the end of every 12 months Scania recommend that the coolant system, the air-cleaner filter element (after 1,200 hours and/or renewing if required), fuel injectors, the electrolyte levels in the batteries as well as cleaning of the batteries and the state of charge in them, the stop function of the engine, and the drive belts are all checked.

Scania also recommend that replacing the lubricating oil, cleaning the oil cleaner, replacing the oil filter, cleaning the coolant system (if required) and replacing of the fuel filter (at 1,200 hours) should be carried out at this time.

At longer intervals they recommend that cleaning the air-cleaner course and safety cartridge, checking/adjusting the valve clearances and renewing (or cleaning) the valve for the closed crankcase ventilation should take place; but owners should refer to the manufacturer's manuals, or the company itself, for further information on these.

The engine number is stamped on the top of the engine block, in front of the first cylinder head under the water pipe, and may also be located on a type plate on the right-hand side behind the oil cleaner. As with Cummins engines, this will help Scania service centres to identify the engine and the relevant parts for it.

Note: on some Scania engine installations, advantage was taken of an engine-mounted hydraulic pump to power the brakes, in which case the gearbox-mounted hydraulic pump and pump drive is no longer required. Similarly an engine-mounted compressor was used to power the gearbox air supply.

Cummins B-series engine

Cummins recommend that the oil level, coolant level, coolant fan, drive belts and fuel-water separator filter are checked on a daily basis.

At every three months, 6,000 miles or 250 hours the engine oil should be changed and the oil filter should be replaced (use Fleetguard LF3349 or equivalent). The air-cleaner restriction and air-intake piping should be inspected, as well as the radiator/intercooler.

ABOVE The Scania DS9 engine installation usually uses new front and rear crossmembers, but the cab wall on the offside of the engine had to be modified. *(John Keohane)*

BELOW At 5.9 litres the Cummins B-series is the smallest engine ever fitted to a Routemaster. It has all-new crossmembers, an integral radiator and intercooler, and, as clearly seen here, the cab wall on the offside of the engine has to be modified. *(Mark Kehoe)*

In addition, at every six months, 12,000 miles or 500 hours the fuel filter should be replaced (use Fleetguard FS1251 or equivalent), and the cooling fan belt tensioner should be checked. The antifreeze should also be checked; Cummins recommends Fleetguard antifreeze coolants for their engines.

At every 12 months, 24,000 miles or 1,000 hours the overhead set should be adjusted to reset valve clearances and a series of tests should be carried out on the drive belts. The air cleaner filter should be inspected and replaced if required (use Fleetguard AF1813 or equivalent).

At every 24 months, 48,000 miles or 2,000 hours the vibration damper rubber, viscous damper and cooling system should also be inspected.

The Cummins manual includes trouble-shooting symptoms charts that are useful when tracking down problems.

The engine data plate is fitted to the nearside of the engine in front of the fuel pump; it includes the ESN (engine serial number) and the CPL (control parts list), which are vital when souring parts from a Cummins agent.

Fuel pump

For the AEC and Leyland engines, two types of in-line fuel pump were fitted, while a CAV DPA distributer (rotary)-type pump was also fitted to some AEC units.

The idling speed on the fuel pump is adjusted once fitted to the vehicle. If this is faulty, pump calibration and testing is best carried out by a specialist once the pump has been removed from the vehicle. Similarly, injectors should be tested and overhauled by a specialist. Once set up, no lubrication is required for the fuel pump, although it should be regularly checked.

Radiator and heating system

It's recommended that the radiator and coolant system should be inspected for wear or damage periodically, both externally and also by flushing through and replacing the antifreeze solution. Also, every few years it's prudent to remove the top heat exchanger and flush through; this can often make the heating system work more efficiently. It's always good practice to regularly check the condition of the pipework and joints to ensure that no leaks have become evident. The antifreeze solution should never be less than 25% and never greater than 50% or frost protection won't be provided as seasonal temperatures drop.

The Clayton heating system fitted as part of the RML refurbishment programme is well known for being problematic, but if it's flushed through and correctly bled it can usually be made to function properly. Another important tip is to clean the fins and vanes in the units themselves, as after more than ten years of use they'll have become full of debris. The stopcocks for the system are fitted in the driver's cab on the nearside wall and under the canopy flap above the bonnet.

Fluid flywheel

In the Llewellyn gland in the original J156 fluid flywheel, the rubber gaiter fitted between the bronze ring and the spacing sleeve hardens over time and becomes ineffective. The main ball bearing race can also wear and result in failure of the gland. The manufacturer of Llewellyn glands has ceased trading and repair kits are consequently becoming hard to find. The availability of these will in time become critical.

The J156 fluid flywheel is common to Routemasters fitted with AEC, Leyland and Iveco engines. Checking the oil level should be carried out with the filler plug at 1½–2 periphery bolts from the TDC – filling the flywheel with the plug at the TDC won't allow adequate expansion of the oil under adverse operating conditions.

Cummins C-series engines were fitted with a number of different types of fluid flywheel. One of these is the Voith TD coupling, which utilises a lip seal instead. Another type is commonly called the Leyland rationalised fluid flywheel. Cummins B-series-engined vehicles have a modern automatic gearbox that incorporates a torque converter, so that the need for a fluid flywheel is eliminated.

Exhaust system

Most Routemasters have the original design of exhaust system fitted, but some have had this replaced with a longer-lasting stainless steel

Eminox system. The Cummins B-series engines have retained the standard rear sections of exhaust, including the silencer, and the exhaust runs along the offside of the vehicle from the engine. An oxidation catalyst supplied by ECS (type AZ29) is mounted in the bay immediately behind the engine. All of the refurbished RMLs and some of the RMs still in service in London in the 21st century had particulate traps fitted at the front of the exhaust system immediately behind the engine.

Standard D182 gearbox

The oil capacity of the standard gearbox should be regularly checked using the gearbox dipstick. This is accessed via the small trap in the centre of the lower passenger saloon floor, using the square shaft of a budget key, or alternatively by unscrewing the four floor screws and lifting the complete gearbox trap. The level of the gear oil should come up to the engraved mark approximately half an inch (13mm) from the bottom of the standard dipstick. The gear cylinder drain plugs should be removed annually and any oil present should be drained off; always ensure that neutral is selected when carrying out this operation. Ensure that the two air-release holes in the electro-pneumatic valve unit aren't blocked.

Gear slip in more than one gear may be due to low air pressure, low battery voltage or a leaking fluid flywheel. If just one gear is slipping, then this may be due to insufficient air pressure, an accumulation of oil in the cylinder and air pipe (which would cause a blockage of the restrictor), leaking piston seals, incorrect brake band or top-speed setting, a leaking solenoid valve, a broken gear band or a failed electrical circuit. The replacement of the piston seals is a relatively easy task and spare seals can still be obtained.

Reports of problems with gearboxes are getting more common. Currently parts are still available and overhauling gearboxes is still possible. It's probable that, as with the brake system, Routemasters simply don't like not being used, and less problems seem to occur when they're used regularly.

It's of the utmost importance that the felt filter in the cab air intake is kept clean, otherwise a slow build-up of air pressure will

occur and the compressor will have a shorter life. The felt element must be replaced and/or dry-cleaned.

Allison gearbox types MT643 and T270

Routemasters fitted with the Cummins B-series engine (and the sole example with the Cummins ISBe engine) no longer have the gearbox fitted midway along the body; instead it's mated to the rear of the engine, and is installed immediately below the trap at the front of the lower passenger saloon that was originally fitted for accessing the fluid flywheel.

There are two types of Allison gearbox fitted to these re-engined vehicles, and the quickest way to tell the difference between them is to check the type of gear selector in the driver's cab. Those with the MT643 gearbox have a cable-controlled Morse quadrant gear selector (positioned to the left of the driver's seat), which has been likened, perhaps unkindly, to that fitted in an automatic Mini Metro from the 1980s, whereas the T270 gearbox has a push-button key pad with a two-digit display. The other way of spotting the T270 installation is that the now disused flywheel cover at the front of the lower passenger saloon has been

ABOVE The EP valve block is mounted on the offside of the gearbox. In front of it is the compressor. Note the particulate filter in the bay in front of the gearbox.
(Mark Kehoe)

modified and reshaped to allow the gearbox to be installed immediately below it.

The transmission fluid can be checked by using the dipstick; this is accessed from above the gearbox via the trap at the front of the lower passenger saloon. It's important that this fluid is maintained at the correct level to ensure efficient operation of the gearbox, as the transmission fluid cools, lubricates and transmits the hydraulic power. The MT643 is a four-speed automatic gearbox with a hydraulic torque converter, a planetary gear train and a hydraulic control system that supplies fluid under pressure to apply the clutch and automatically change gear. Allison recommend that the transmission fluid for the MT643 is changed at 25,000 miles or every 12 months (whichever comes sooner), and the filters should be changed at the same time. Note: these intervals can be extended if TranSynd or TES 295 approved fluid is used instead of the usual Dexron.

It's important to check the old transmission fluid for dirt, coolant contamination or any metal particles that may be evidence of problems with the gearbox itself.

The installation and access points for the T270 are identical to those for the MT643 gearbox. It was the replacement for the MT643 and became available during the refurbishment programme, in about 2002. It has similar characteristics to the latter but is fully electronic, which enhances its shift quality and smoothness of operation. Allison anticipate a life of between three and five years for the transmission fluid and filters, but this will depend on the type of filter fitted and the operation of the vehicle.

TranSynd or TES 295 approved fluid should be used in this transmission as standard, although a TES 389 approved fluid can be used for some operating conditions; further advice should be sought from Allison Transmission or their agents. Generally, if a TES 389 fluid is used then the fluid and the filters should be changed more frequently (with intervals as low as 20,000 miles, 500 hours or every six months, whichever comes soonest).

With the revised transmissions, a tandem hydraulic pump is located on the engine front gear train accessory drive to supply the brakes and power steering.

Suspension

On the original AEC and Leyland-engined vehicles, the grease nipples on the cross-shafts mounted on the steering box and front engine crossmember should be charged with grease at every service. All fork ends should also be oiled at every service.

The upper kingpin swivels should also be charged with grease at every service. The thrust buttons should be lubricated with EP90 or equivalent oil via the bottom bush. The wishbone bearings should be checked for any deterioration. At every annual service the hub bearings should be repacked with grease and the end-float should be reset.

The rubber washers and bushes at the top and bottom of the front and rear suspension dampers should be checked for wear at each service. If they're cracked, worn or show evidence of movement, they should be replaced. The bump and rebound stops for the front and rear suspensions should be examined for wear and to check that they're not missing. If necessary they should be replaced.

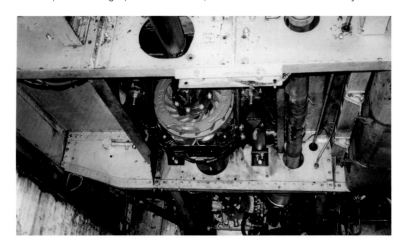

If a damper is found to be losing oil, it should be removed and replaced or overhauled. It's recommended that you shouldn't simply add oil, as special fluid and parts are likely to be required.

The RMC, RCL and RMA types used air for the bellows-type rear suspension, but many vehicles have been converted to standard coil springs and have had this equipment removed.

Rear axle

Three differential ratios are fitted to suit service conditions, with the corresponding speedo transmitter drive, as follows:

■ The DU17 is the standard RM and RML differential for town service conditions. It has a 5.22:1 ratio, and is fitted with the speedo-transmitted drive pinion with 11 teeth.
■ The DU18 is the RMC differential for Green Line work. It has a 4.77:1 ratio and is fitted with the speedo-transmitted drive pinion with 12 teeth.
■ The DU24 is the RCL and BEA (RMA) differential for Green Line and express airways services. It has a 4.08:1 ratio and is fitted with the speedo-transmitted drive pinion with 14 teeth.

The 50 RMFs built for Northern General were fitted with a worm-drive axle of 5.2:1 ratio.

The differential should be checked for oil level by removing the brass filler plug and ensuring that the oil is level with the top of the filler neck.

At a major service the rear hubs should be checked for oil content (bellows gland type) or regreased if lip-type seals are fitted. An early bellows gland hub oil seal may be identified by the hexagonal oil level/filler plug adjacent to the wheel flange. Later buses have grease-lubricated hubs with lip-type seals fitted at the inboard and outboard ends of the hubs.

Check for oil contamination from leaks around the brake linings as this may well indicate that the hub seals should be replaced on that side.

Wheels

The torque setting for wheel nuts is 400–450lb/ft. When refitting wheels, always oil the threads on the studs, and never paint the threads or the wheel nut cones in the wheel centre.

Steering

The steering box oil level should be checked and topped up at six-monthly or annual service, depending on the operation of the vehicle. All ten steering linkage ball joints should be greased at each service. The two relay lever points must be lubricated with engine oil at each service. A steering column damper is fitted to some RMC, RCL and RMA vehicles, and the condition of this as well as its mountings should be checked at each service. The header tank for the power steering should be checked and topped up if necessary; the level is indicated by the sight-tube on the side of the tank.

Subframes

All frame connections to the A-frame and B-frame should be checked for tightness at every service. The Panhard rod and pivot bush rubber bearings on the B-frame should be checked for wear.

Brakes

One of the unique features of the Routemaster is its hydraulic braking system with accumulators. At every service the brake cylinders, valves, hoses and fittings should all be examined for leaks. London Transport carried out a strict routine of tests, originally at six-week intervals. To an enthusiastic amateur without specialist gauges, a 'K-9' intensifier (see Glossary), appropriate understanding of the system and mechanical competency, the Routemaster hydraulic braking system is perceived as the vehicle's Achilles heel. If you *do* have the equipment and competence to check the air pre-charge pressure or to

Recharging the brakes

(all Mark Kehoe, except where indicated):

RIGHT After fully discharging the system, unscrew the dust caps from the accumulators...

FAR RIGHT ...to reveal the Schrader valves.

RIGHT Screw on the hose from the intensifier...

FAR RIGHT ...connect the intensifier to the compressor...

recharge the accumulators, then always remember to fully discharge the system first. Also, always use a clean, dry air supply, although nitrogen was actually used by a number of companies, including Northern General and Clydeside Scottish.

London Transport also used to replace the header tank filter at intervals of two years, but this is now rarely carried out. The filter is easy to source and change, and *should* be changed if at all possible (use Fleetguard LF563 or equivalent).

The biggest error made when working on a

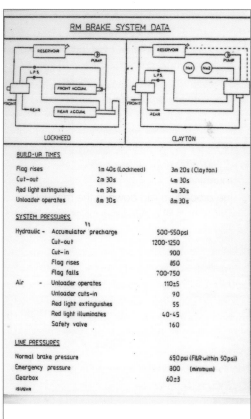

RM BRAKE SYSTEM DATA

LOCKHEED | CLAYTON

BUILD-UP TIMES

	Lockheed	Clayton
Flag rises	1m 40s (Lockheed)	3m 20s (Clayton)
Cut-out	2m 30s	4m 30s
Red light extinguishes	4m 30s	4m 30s
Unloader operates	8m 30s	8m 30s

SYSTEM PRESSURES

Hydraulic -	Accumulator precharge	500-550psi
	Cut-out	1200-1250
	Cut-in	900
	Flag rises	850
	Flag falls	700-750
Air -	Unloader operates	110±5
	Unloader cuts-in	90
	Red light extinguishes	55
	Red light illuminates	40-45
	Safety valve	160

LINE PRESSURES

Normal brake pressure	650psi (F&R within 50psi)
Emergency pressure	800 (minimum)
Gearbox	60±3

ISI/GVR

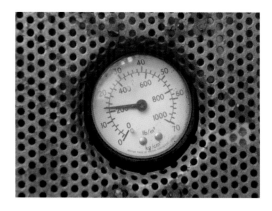

RIGHT ...and recharge the system so that a minimum pre-charge of 500lb/in^2 is achieved. Repeat for the other accumulator.

FAR RIGHT Brake chart. *(London Transport)*

ROUTEMASTER BUS MANUAL

FAR LEFT Following the manual, the operation of the brake system can be further checked with the aid of gauges...

LEFT ...connected to the test points on the offside front of the front boat.

FAR LEFT The pump drive unit should be regularly greased and the belts correctly tensioned to avoid the drive seizing and the quill drive breaking and failing.

LEFT Spare compressor belts should be wired to the crossmember in front of the gearbox.

Routemaster is putting brake fluid in the brake system – this should *never* be done; *always* use the correct hydraulic fluid. It shouldn't be necessary to ever change the oil used in the system, unless it's been contaminated.

When the white light and/or red warning flag shows, the vehicle should be stopped and the engine revved up in neutral for 30 seconds. If either the brake or gearbox indicators fail to respond further instruction or assistance should be sought.

The procedure laid down in the manual for checking the brake system involves checking the build-up times, racing, and idling times. As a rule of thumb, if you're waiting too long for the flag to rise after the engine is started then there's probably a problem in the system. Once the system is fully charged the fluid level on the header tank should be at the 'F' (full) mark. When discharged the oil should occupy the full volume of the tank. Never top up the tank with the system charged, otherwise when discharged the oil could overflow. Access to the tank is via the flap on the offside of the vehicle adjacent to the driver's step.

The microswitches on the brake and gearbox lines can become stuck and are quite often the cause of a warning light coming on, but they can be relatively easily replaced and repaired.

The brake lever assembly should be greased at each service, and the operating links oiled. The automatic brake adjuster unit should be lubricated using graphited engine oil, at brake-liner change only, via the oil nipple.

The brake adjusters should be checked at each service. If the clearance is incorrect then fierce or uneven braking will occur. The adjusters should be greased at each service,

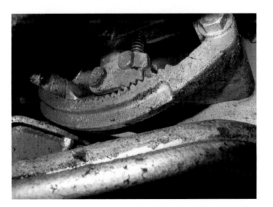

LEFT The teeth wear on the handbrake ratchet and pawl, with the eventual result that the handbrake won't hold. *(Mark Kehoe)*

RIGHT The oil level in the compressor should be regularly checked to avoid it seizing.
(Mark Kehoe)

and the operating links oiled. The brake camshafts should also be given one shot of grease at every service. The four clevis pins should be brushed with graphited oil.

The three handbrake relay brackets should also be greased at each service. The cross shaft should be greased and the nine brake linkage pins should be brushed with graphited oil. The pawl and quadrant, located at the bottom of the handbrake lever, should receive a small quantity of grease. Note that operation of the handbrake without fully pulling up the release handle will result in wear of the teeth

BELOW Above the compressor is the brake pump.
(Mark Kehoe)

on the pawl and quadrant, and eventually failure of the handbrake mechanism.

The brake-pedal pad should be inspected and replaced if missing or severely worn.

Air system

Adjustment of the compressor belt drive is achieved by amending the location of the mounting bracket. Spare belts can be tied to the adjacent body crossmember by removing the prop shafts and placing them over it.

The compressor should be checked at every service and topped up with engine oil to the level of the filler neck opening. Should oil consumption increase, this is a sign that problems are likely to occur and further investigation should be undertaken. The safety valve should be removed from the compressor delivery port once a year and the plunger checked.

The air reservoir tank was upgraded in later refurbishments but the principle remains the same. After first exhausting the system of air by repeated selection and disengagement of a gear, the drain plug in the air reservoir should be removed at every service to release any accumulation of moisture. Check the filter in the unloader valve. The reducer valve should be checked at a major service.

Electrics

London Transport carried out set electrical testing to check the charging systems and circuits. As most vehicles have been rewired it's unlikely that these tests are still valid, but testing by a competent commercial electrical engineer at regular intervals is recommended.

Modern alternators don't require any maintenance, but some of the old alternators have Stauffer grease cups that should be filled and reapplied at each major service; however, care should be taken not to over-lubricate any of the older type fitted with Tecalemit nipples. If the alternator is noisy, it should be removed for overhaul and replaced. The alternator belts fitted will vary depending on the type of alternator, but the belt tension should be checked to allow ½in (13mm) deflection at the centre of each belt. If one belt is showing signs of stretch then all three should be replaced.

The starter motor should be inspected at each annual service.

The standard SCG and CAV automatic gearbox control panels were replaced as part of the RML refurbishment programme, and at the fitment of the later Allison gearboxes. For the original set-up, there are a number of tests that can be applied if, for example, a particular gear fails to engage or if no gears can be engaged at all. A common fault is when third and fourth gear can't be engaged, which usually indicates failure of the speed signal generator. All such failures can be detected using a gearbox test unit, but in the likely unavailability of one of these there are a number of readings that can be taken across the terminals which should give specific readings depending on the conditions found.

The original manual provides details of the way the test equipment was used, as well as the road-test procedure to be adopted. It also gives a guide to fault diagnosis for various typical conditions encountered.

The replacement gearbox control panel fitted during the RML refurbishment programme to suit Cummins C-series and Iveco-engined vehicles was the CAV551 unit. This has proved to be very reliable and was also fitted to some RMs re-engined with Scania units in the late 1990s. However, it's not interchangeable with the earlier installations carried out during the RML refurbishment programme.

The CAV551 gear control panels were fitted as a modern component to provide a throttle dip feature during gearchanges. The panel was designed to reduce gearbox wear by smoother

ABOVE Refurbished RMLs were fitted with a speed sensor ahead of the differential in place of the original transmitter mounted to the rear of the gearbox. *(Mark Kehoe)*

gearchanges, and thereby extend gearbox life. The panel incorporated a starter interlock to prevent the bus being started unless it's in neutral gear. Although some of these features can be removed or disabled, advice should be sought before working on any of them unless you're knowledgeable and/or competent in these areas.

By the adoption of a bypass plug the original automatic gearbox control panel can be bypassed and the gearbox operated in manual mode. Many owners prefer to drive their vehicles in manual as it gives them more control.

The original driver's cab electrical equipment was partially updated during the RML refurbishment programme and totally replaced during the later refurbishments by Marshall. Both programmes involved total rewiring of vehicles, and local refurbishment programmes subsequently carried out by some operators has included partial rewiring. However, if the original equipment is still fitted it's likely that the original aluminium wiring remains intact too. If it is, it's likely to be degrading by now and will become a serious problem over the next few years. It was originally installed to save weight, but the aluminium is now simply too old. The same is true of the circuits for the interior lighting, the destination lighting, and the bell/buzzer. Generally failures due to the age of the cabling, connections, insulation and weather seals are

likely to become an increasing problem as vehicles get older.

Other areas that should be checked at major services include the original-style Arens engine stop control switch, which may require adjustment and should be greased at the fuel pump end at every service. The wiper, headlights, destination lights, fog light (if fitted) and sidelights are controlled by traditional switches that may fail due to old age, but can be repaired. The early type of direction indicator switch with a large red top was mostly replaced by a newer Lucas unit. The contacts in the older units are more temperamental but can be repaired. Note: the wiring to the direction indicators is in series; whilst the wiring can be converted to a parallel arrangement, the system then can't detect a bulb failure, and this arrangement is therefore illegal in the UK.

The original-style wiper requires a minimum of maintenance and simply needs to be lubricated with grease. However, the drive is known to wear and replacement parts are now hard to obtain, so most vehicles that remain in service have had modern Britax units fitted.

It's important to check the batteries on a regular basis. Using only distilled or de-ionised water to top-up the cells, you should smear all connections with petroleum jelly, keep them clean (including removing and cleaning the complete battery tray), repaint with anti-sulphuric paint at regular intervals, and if the vehicle is to be left for more than four weeks, apply a 'trickle-charge'.

Bodywork

Items for inspection and lubrication within the bodywork include:

- All budget locks to blind boxes, floor traps, battery door under the stairs, brake reservoir, number-plate light and ticket bins.
- Driver's cab windscreen.
- Driver's cab door, including the signalling window.
- Driver's cab emergency exit, the rear (upper deck) emergency exit and the lower deck offside emergency exit on RMLs.

- All window winders – the nipples should be charged with a small amount of grease on major servicing.
- Mechanism to destination equipment.
- Bonnet hinges and handle.
- Security of the seat frames.

Obtaining spare parts

With the demise of the main London fleets there's no longer a large number of operational Routemasters for which stocks of parts need to be manufactured and stored in order to keep hundreds of vehicles operational 24 hours a day, seven days a week and 12 months a year. There used to be companies that specialised in manufacturing and supplying component parts for the 600-plus Routemasters in London, but as demand for component spares has dropped dramatically these companies no longer maintain stocks. In most cases the parts are still available, but there has been an inevitable increase in prices, and smaller stocks – if any – are kept 'on the shelf'. The companies that are still operating Routemasters have their own supply chain, and also probably hold stock of the most common parts that they might require.

A problem, if that's the right way to describe it, for other people in this climate of diminishing availability is that many owners – whether new or people that have been involved with Routemasters for many years – have acquired their own stock of parts for a 'rainy day', and by hoarding these spares are in effect exacerbating the shortages.

For the first 20 years of Routemaster ownership outside London Transport, only the standard non-refurbished Routemaster was available. These were generally AEC-engined, with some Leyland-engined examples, and all had original electrical systems and fittings. (Details of the original classification coding system are included in Appendix 4.) However, from 2003 onwards RMs and RMLs became available in large quantities with Cummins, Iveco and Scania engines. Later examples became available with a second type of Cummins engine and, for the first time, two types of modern Allison gearboxes.

Suddenly the requirements for Routemaster

ABOVE Don't forget to lubricate all of the various budget locks, including the one over the rear registration plate. *(Mark Kehoe)*

spares entered a whole new era, with original Routemasters versus refurbished Routemasters. Up until this time the London Transport manuals had been sufficient for maintenance purposes, as they contained all the reference systems that London Transport had used. But now a complete new system of component parts applied, the original manual was almost useless, and a comprehensive parts manual for the Routemaster no longer existed. But worse than that, it soon became clear that each company that had owned and operated the vehicles had applied not only their own maintenance procedures but had also modified the vehicles in different ways. An example of such complications is that although three operating companies had fitted the Scania engine conversion, all three conversions were different and they had been fitted by up to five different companies or workshops, so that it was highly unlikely there was a 'standard' bus or conversion!

On the positive side, however, the majority of these new components could still be sourced from major manufacturers and industry networks – for example, Cummins would support the C-series and then the B-series engines, as would Scania with the DS9 engine and the Iveco Ford group with the Iveco 836/1 engine.

More difficult to find were some of the original components needed to restore these refurbished vehicle back to original condition, if only in cosmetic appearance – for example, front and rear light units. If the intention of a restorer is to rebuild a Routemaster to fully original condition it must be understood from the outset that, as the years go by, it's getting more and more difficult to repair the rarer units such as alternators and fuel pumps, for which the components are no longer available.

Although some companies are still able to supply parts for Routemasters, it has become common practice for individual owners or groups of owners to attempt to take matters into their own hands and source parts themselves. Often these plans are carried out with the best of intentions, to resolve a specific problem or get a vehicle back on the road, but it's always important to understand which parts are in the 'safety critical' category, and not try to reinvent what's already been invented.

Small items that have been produced by such individuals or organisations include battery box covers, handbrake ratchet and pawls, budget 'T' keys, indicator ear rubbers, coil springs, front wheel trim, rear 'dustbin lid' wheel trim, headlight trim, timber platform edges, bodywork fixing screws and inserts, indicator-ear mounting brackets, interior light bulbs, interior light fittings, rear light boxes, radiator badges, bonnet badges, window rubber, B-frame sandwich rubbers and even engine mounts.

It has thus become more important than ever that owners keep in contact with each other in order to communicate current stock levels

for parts, so that if a problem area is identified action can be taken. In 1988 the Routemaster Operators' & Owners' Association – now usually referred to simply as the Routemaster Association – was formed, and one of its aspirations has always been to share technical experience, information and parts availability. It's the ideal medium through which to deal with such problems; it's kept informed by its members and is able to react quickly in distributing the information. Over the years the Association has been fairly successful at carrying out this function, but there are also other ways that Routemaster owners have been able to resolve their problems and keep their vehicles on the road.

Several options are available regarding the next course of action to take. A number of owners working together is immediately beneficial from a purchasing point of view, and also facilitates the sharing of information. The worst possible outcome is that a part thus manufactured is then not wanted, and just sits on a shelf in some store shed awaiting an eventual need somewhere.

An example of a present part requirement is that for half-shafts. There are minimal or no stocks available anywhere, and there are some vehicles that have been cannibalised and now require them again. To have them manufactured would cost many thousands of pounds to produce just a small batch, and such an expense would not be affordable to the average owner. To date insufficient owners have come forward

RIGHT The finishing touches – don't forget to refit the front wheel trim; they can even be fitted to the single-piece wheels, as seen here. *(Mark Kehoe)*

anyway requiring a pair of half-shafts, and some vehicles consequently remain off the road.

The conclusion has to be that either suppliers should be encouraged to restock such items, if demand can be shown to exist, or alternatively that groups of owners requiring the same part should come together until there are sufficient of them to bear the cost of production. With today's communication methods, emails and the Internet it should be possible to advertise that somebody requires a particular part or intends to have it manufactured. Website-based forums are a particularly good method of communication, and owners participating in these can often obtain an almost instant reply and resolution to their own particular problem.

Items wanted or for sale can also be advertised in this way – the days of advertising in a magazine that may take weeks to print and distribute are long gone. Web-based auction sites such as eBay are another way of purchasing parts, but owners using them should always beware, as prices can be very high and there's usually no guarantee or warranty available with such purchases.

ABOVE If it all goes wrong a tow home might be necessary. Don't forget to make sure that the half-shafts have been disconnected. *(Andrew Morgan)*

BELOW Before fully hydraulic tow trucks were available, special A-frames were bolted to the front of the A-frame and the vehicle would be lifted at the front if lifting was required. Nowadays the only acceptable way to tow a Routemaster is by utilising a front lift and lifting with the correct forks. Note: the safety chains hadn't yet been fitted when this photograph was taken. *(Andrew Morgan)*

Chapter Five

Routemaster in the 21st century

Where to find and ride a Routemaster

Since the withdrawal of Routemasters from mainstream service in London at the end of 2005 they have been confined to small-scale operations. So if you want to sample a Routemaster and ride on one, where can you find them?

OPPOSITE A Transport for London Routemaster on Heritage route 15 in London. *(Mark Kehoe)*

ABOVE From the outside this looks like a standard refurbished Routemaster from the batch completed by Marshall Bus in 2001–2, but this is actually the unique Euro III-engined vehicle. Although there were alternative future ideas at prototype stage, including an LPG-powered version, RM1562 was fitted with the Cummins iSBE Euro III, Allison T270 and Telma axial retarder, and has now been in continual service since the end of 2002. This was possibly the furthest that development of the Routemaster reached before it fell out of favour. However, European emission standards continue to challenge engine designers and manufacturers, and vehicle operators still wish to use Routemasters in major cities. In London the Low Emission Zone (LEZ) has an exemption clause that can be applied to Routemasters, but elsewhere experiments have been taking place to upgrade a Euro II-engined Routemaster to Euro V. *(Andrew Morgan)*

ABOVE The refurbished RMs have many unique features including modern square-style rear lights, hopper windows and yellow reshaped platform handrails. RM871 was sold by London Buses in 1988, only to be reacquired in 2000 after it had seen service with two other operators. *(Mark Kehoe)*

BELOW Two Heritage routes operate in London seven days a week, numbered as route 9 and route 15. They use a total of ten of the refurbished RMs. RM1933 has carried many special paint schemes and in autumn 2009 it was repainted back to this splendid recreation of 1933 London Transport livery. *(Andrew Morgan)*

As we saw back in Chapter 1, since November 2005 two Heritage routes in Central London have been operated daily, initially at 15-minute intervals, by ten refurbished Routemasters, with five each working on shortened versions of routes 9 and 15. The full-length version of routes 9 and 15 served by modern low-floor buses operate in parallel to these Heritage routes. At the end of 2010 these services were slightly revised and now operate at 15- or 20-minute intervals between approximately 09:30 and 18:30, seven days a week, as follows:

- Route 9 operates at 20-minute intervals from Kensington High Street to Trafalgar Square via the Royal Albert Hall, Knightsbridge, Hyde Park Corner and Piccadilly Circus, and is operated by First London.
- Route 15 operates at 15-minute intervals from Trafalgar Square to Tower Hill via Monument, St Paul's Cathedral and Aldwych, and is operated by East London (part of the Stagecoach group).

The Routemasters used were refurbished in 2001 as part of the Transport *for* London (TfL) refurbishment programme, which included the fitment of Euro II engines, and they remain owned by Transport *for* London.

In addition to these Heritage services, a

small sightseeing operation around London is operated by Premium Tours using two open-top RMLs and one open-top RM. As with the Heritage routes, the Routemasters used are Euro II examples, but these particular vehicles were converted for London United and Metroline in 2002–3 as part of separate refurbishment programmes.

An even smaller operation is the Ghost Bus Tour that operates in Central London in the evenings using either an RM or an RML in black livery.

Another sightseeing service that uses Routemasters is the Mac City Tour in Edinburgh. This operates from early April to

late December, using up to seven different Routemasters that have been rebuilt for their new role. The total Mac Tours fleet currently comprises ten extended ERMs, two RCLs and one RM. Out of these, two of the ERMs together with the two RCLs and the RM have been converted to part open-top. All of the ERMs and the RM have had new doors fitted to their platforms, and all vehicles are fitted with Euro II engines. Mac Tours is actually the largest Routemaster operator providing a regular passenger service in the Untied Kingdom.

Though these are the main Routemaster operations still to be found, the vehicle's popularity has encouraged the acquisition of numerous examples by various companies around the country for private hire and corporate contract work, and they can often be seen being used for weddings. Generally all have retained red-based paintwork resembling London Transport's traditional livery.

The majority of these operations are, not surprisingly, based around London and the south-east of England, but they're also found as far afield as Cornwall in the south-west and Edinburgh in the north. The largest such operator is Hertfordshire-based Timebus Travel, with 13 operational Routemasters available for hire or contract work.

Because the use of most such vehicles is confined to hire and contract work it's generally not possible to ride on them. However, occasionally they can be seen operating on special services, such as the examples mentioned below. Alternatively they might participate in seasonal operations from time to time. Examples include Dreadnought Coaches in Alnwick in Northumberland, Scottish Travel in Greenock near Glasgow in Scotland, Western Greyhound in Cornwall, and Local Haunts in Portsmouth, Hampshire. Once again, the majority of these operate in London red livery.

The Go Ahead London commercial fleet is regularly used during the summer, and their Routemasters are often seen running special

ABOVE LEFT Wedding transport has become a popular new use for Routemasters, especially around the London area. Here an early RML is in use with the Kent-based London Bus Company. *(Andrew Morgan)*

ABOVE Essex-based Ensign Bus (rendered 'Ensignbus' on the side of their vehicles) have at least one of each type of Routemaster within their heritage fleet, and most are operational at any one time. RM54, seen here on a wedding hire, was also the last operational RM on route 159 on 9 December 2005. *(Andrew Morgan)*

LEFT RM371 was acquired by Ensign Bus after use by Mac Tours and Kelvin Scottish. It was converted to open-top, re-engined, and had platform doors fitted by Mac Tours. Note the LED tail lights fitted in place of the original units. *(Andrew Morgan)*

BELOW LEFT One of the more unusual Routemaster variants is the former BEA front-entrance Routemaster. Pristine RMA37 has been owned by Timebus Travel of St Albans since 1996, and during this time it has been re-engined with a Cummins Euro II. *(Andrew Morgan)*

BELOW RIGHT With 14 vehicles, including six RMLs, Timebus Travel is the largest operator of Routemasters in the UK. RML2310 has a Cummins C-series engine, the clue to which is the original-sized radiator seen through the grille. *(Andrew Morgan)*

services on Derby Day, as well as to the Chelsea flower show, the Hampton Court flower show and the Wimbledon tennis championships.

The South Devon Railway use RM1872 for their service from the railway centre at Buckfastleigh to the town and to Buckfast Abbey, but only if the weather is likely to be inclement or the usual vehicle, a former Devon General open-top AEC Regent V, isn't available.

An unusual operation is the use of Routemasters on London Underground railway replacement services; although these operations are now officially to be 100% low-floor vehicles, a Routemaster can still be seen when other vehicles aren't available. Sullivan Buses from Hertfordshire have been known to supply one of their Routemasters for services in north-west London.

And don't forget that outside the United Kingdom there are approximately 600 Routemasters that can be found in at least 59 countries. The largest collections of these are in Canada, where they serve with two sizeable operators. One of these, Absolute Charters Inc of Halifax in Nova Scotia, operates 26 Routemasters, which makes it the largest operational Routemaster fleet in the world, and twice as big as any of the operations in the UK.

Museums, rallies and running days

So where else can you see or ride on a Routemaster?

As will be seen in the Epilogue, a number of museums have Routemasters within their collections, which can be viewed either as part of a static collection or, sometimes, in action at events and museum open days. In some museums it's possible to see vehicles being worked on or undergoing restoration.

The London Transport Museum Depot at Acton holds the majority of the museum's collection that isn't on display in the main museum in Covent Garden. However, it's only open to the general public on selected dates throughout the year, including themed open weekends. This purpose-built facility provides 6,000m^2 of storage space in secure, environmentally controlled conditions. Among the many vehicles it holds are prototypes RM1 and 2, fully-restored Green Line RCL2229, and the unique front-entrance FRM1. RM2 is currently undergoing long-term restoration within the Depot to take it back to original condition. RM1 is occasionally used at events or services connected with various anniversaries. The FRM was previously used on such occasions as well, but hasn't been seen in passenger service since the Routemaster 50 anniversary celebration in 2004.

Cobham Bus Museum has the third

prototype, RML3, and Green Line liveried RMC1461 as part of its collection. As well as being seen on regular services to and from the museum and at museum-associated events, they're regularly used on special services around the London area.

It's rare to find a vehicle rally in South-East England without at least one Routemaster in attendance. The big rallies such as Showbus often attract more than 40, with most variants and types being represented. In fact with Routemasters now in private ownership all across the country it's not unusual to find one attending an event almost anywhere.

ABOVE RT8 beside RM140 provides an interesting comparison between a 1939 London bus and a 1959 London bus at the Colindale running day at the RAF Museum in August 2010. RM140 has an early body with non-opening upper-deck windows. *(Mark Kehoe)*

BELOW LEFT Running days recreate routes from years gone by, and immaculate RM1069 is seen here departing from Colindale to operate over route 221. *(Mark Kehoe)*

LEFT In as-withdrawn condition, this is RML2394 at the annual Amersham Running Day in October 2005, having just operated route 353. It has subsequently been repainted into original livery and has regained original indicator 'ears'. *(Andrew Morgan)*

LEFT A running day occurs every few years over the two Heritage routes in central London. The operation sees additional vehicles running across both routes joined together; hence this First London RM is completing a run westbound on route 15 and will then continue running westwards on route 9. RM1650, repainted back into its 1977 Silver Jubilee livery, normally operates on route 9 only occasionally. *(Andrew Morgan)*

BELOW Road-runs across old routes often take place with varying numbers of usually privately-owned vehicles. In this case the vehicles from the 2011 Route 2 run are all parked together after successfully completing the journey from Golders Green to Crystal Palace. *(Andrew Morgan)*

BELOW A road-run over route 88 in central London sees two RMs and two RMLs pausing for a photographic stop en route. *(Mark Kehoe)*

BELOW RIGHT RM8 was sold for preservation in 1985. It has since regained its original-style advertisements from the 1958 Commercial Motor Show. *(Andrew Morgan)*

ABOVE RM44 was sold in 1985 and subsequently passed through the hands of several owners, including two operators. It was secured for preservation in 2000 and was returned to colourful Southend Transport livery. *(Andrew Morgan)*

ABOVE RM158 was sold in 1985 and has passed through six owners. It is presently preserved with the flake grey relief band used from the late 1960s to the early 1970s. *(Andrew Morgan)*

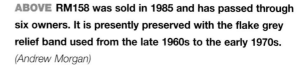

LEFT RM254 became a garage Showbus in 1981 before being sold for preservation in 1985. During the 1980s and 1990s its immaculate condition earned it a reputation for being a prizewinner wherever it went. *(Andrew Morgan)*

BELOW LEFT RM308 was sold in 1985 and acquired for preservation in 1987. It's unusual, as it's one of the 100 bodies built with opening upper deck windows and the ventilation slots fitted above them – the latter can be distinguished by the 'eyebrows' above the front windows, visible below the beading beneath the roof dome. *(Mark Kehoe)*

BELOW RM737 was another garage Showbus from the early 1980s that became well known around the rally circuit during the 1980s and 1990s. It was also the first standard RM to be sold for preservation from London Transport in 1983. *(Mark Kehoe)*

ABOVE RM1414 was loaned to Manchester Corporation Transport for demonstration in 1963 and upon withdrawal 20 years later it was donated to the Greater Manchester Museum of Transport, where it is seen operating in connection with events at the museum. *(Andrew Morgan)*

ABOVE RM1699 was sold to Stagecoach in 1987, for whom it briefly operated in Glasgow before passing into preservation. It is now immaculately presented in original as-new 1960s livery. *(Mark Kehoe)*

LEFT Two not so immaculate RMs, but ignoring their external appearance there are numerous detail differences between them. *(Mark Kehoe)*

BELOW LEFT The Shillibeer colour scheme of 1979 is an attractive livery to which two RMs have been restored, RM2186 being the more recent example to have been completed. *(Andrew Morgan)*

BELOW RMC1469 was withdrawn from passenger service by London Country in 1980 and became a training bus until 1995. It was latterly fitted out internally as a classroom. By the summer of 1999 it had been restored to near-original condition and has been seen at events for several years, carrying passengers again, including on running days. *(Andrew Morgan)*

FAR LEFT Two RMCs together, but in different liveries. On the left is the original Green Line livery and on the right the 1970s National Bus Company livery. The spelling on the destination blind on RMC1476 is a correct representation from 1980. (Mark Kehoe)

A more recent and successful attraction, often as an alternative to traditional rallies or events, has been the 'running day'. Instead of the familiar static events with vehicles just parked up, these feature vehicles in motion, operating on or recreating routes on which they can be ridden by enthusiasts and general public alike. Depending on the theme for the event, Routemasters are regularly seen taking part in these, although most running days involving Routemasters are inevitably in the London and Home Counties area. Themes can be focused on a particular area or type of vehicle. A minor exception to the general 'London and Home Counties area' rule has been operator Western Greyhound, who have four Routemasters and have organised events in the Newquay area of Cornwall, as well as including their standard RM, open-top RM, RML and RMA in use on their routes alongside other vehicles.

ABOVE RIGHT The detail of the original platform doors and emergency exit compares with the earlier photograph of RM371 on page 135. (Mark Kehoe)

LEFT This RMC is in the 1970s London Country colour scheme that predated the National Bus Company livery; it has lost its brake cooling grilles, and has the later radiator grille, albeit with a blank badge. However, due to a change in registration this is actually RMC1500, numbered as RMC1486 to match its new registration. (Mark Kehoe)

LEFT RMC1507 was the first example of its class to be preserved (in 1981). It stands out amongst almost uninterrupted lines of red Routemasters. (Mark Kehoe)

ABOVE RCL2260 beside RMC1486 makes an interesting study of the frontal differences and changes. To add to the minutiae, the RCL has been fitted with modern mirrors and windscreen, and is missing its fog light. *(Mark Kehoe)*

ABOVE The rear of RCL2260 in near-original condition. It carries the wording 'Blue Triangle' in the roundel rather than 'Green Line', and also modern-style emergency exit stickers, as it was part of the Blue Triangle operational fleet. *(Mark Kehoe)*

ABOVE The rear of RMC1486. The transfer on the lower rear nearside corner confirms the lower seating capacity of the RMCs, with their more comfortable seats and improved spacing. *(Mark Kehoe)*

LEFT London Transport Museum restored RCL2229 after it was donated to the collection in 1985. Apart from the missing fog light it's in original condition. *(Andrew Morgan)*

BELOW With the availability of RMLs for the first time after 2003, a few have reverted back to variations of London Country livery. This was one of the more rare liveries from the early 1970s before the adoption of National Bus Company colours, and includes the 'flying polo' symbol. *(Andrew Morgan)*

BELOW RML2412 has been restored to another 1970s livery with non-underlined fleet names, grey wheels and yellow relief band. This restoration has gone a stage further than most and has had an AEC engine reinstated under the bonnet. *(Mark Kehoe)*

ABOVE Retaining its Iveco engine, RML2514 has reverted to the livery of Kentish Bus that it wore between 1993 and 1998 for the tendered operation of route 19. *(Andrew Morgan)*

BELOW One of the earliest Routemasters to be preserved is Northern General 2105. It carries original livery and has been in preservation with the same owner for over 30 years. *(Andrew Morgan)*

RIGHT Any major rally in the London area can attract a large number of Routemasters. Cobham Bus Museum has their major event at the beginning of April every year, with a line-up of Routemasters of just about every variant on display. *(Mark Kehoe)*

BELOW RML3 makes its debut with its restored front, and the photographers await their turn to get their shot. *(Mark Kehoe)*

LEFT RML2613 has been restored externally to the 1980s livery of white relief band with white roundel and district symbol. *(Andrew Morgan)*

BELOW RCL2233 arriving at the Routemaster 50 celebration at Finsbury Park in 2004 to join the uninterrupted line-up of Routemasters. *(Mark Kehoe)*

Preserving Routemasters

In the final years of mainstream Routemaster operation in London, sales of Routemasters to individuals as the ultimate 'must-have' fashion accessory and the ultimate big boy's toy were very common. Now, over five years later, many of these Routemasters have been resold as full realisation of what had been acquired became apparent.

OPPOSITE Having already been the last AEC-engined bus in regular service in September 2004, RM5 later performed the last crew-operated journey on route 38 in October 2005. *(Andrew Morgan)*

ABOVE Fast forward to 1983, and the end of the era of garage Showbuses; RM1563 was restored in early 1981 to original 1963 condition and is caught entering Mortlake garage.
(Malcolm Irvine)

RIGHT Concorde was withdrawn from passenger service in October 2003 after 34 years of flight, but the Routemaster lives on. In this shot Concorde 01 and RM1 are posed at Duxford in September 2004 as part of the Routemaster's 50th anniversary celebrations that summer.
(Andrew Morgan)

Howether, the fact that they had been bought in the first place meant that – unlike previous classes of bus that were replaced and withdrawn virtually anywhere in the United Kingdom – most Routemasters were indeed saved following withdrawal, and although some (and more as the years have gone by) have been exported, the vast majority have remained in the United Kingdom. Several dealers were involved in the sale of the London fleets, but Essex-based Ensign Bus handled the majority of all Routemaster sales during this period.

As the Routemaster was the last London Transport-designed, traditional, open rear-platform bus, large numbers of this popular vehicle have passed into preservation. All four original prototypes survive today. Leyland-engined RM3 was the first to be sold for preservation, passing to the Cobham Bus Museum, while RM1 and RM2 were donated to the London Transport Museum and Leyland-engined RMC4 passed via various owners to the London Bus Company in Kent. The unique front-entrance rear-engined Routemaster, FRM1, was also donated to the London Transport Museum and arrived the year before RM1 and RM2 in 1984. Of these, none are on permanent display alas, but, as explained above, since 1999 vehicles in the London Transport Museum collection which aren't on display at Covent Garden are stored at the museum's Depot at Acton.

RCL2229 and RM1737 were donated to the London Transport Museum in April 1985 and January 1986 respectively. Since December 1993 RM1737 has been on display at the London Transport Museum at Covent Garden.

Other Routemasters sold for preservation in the mid-1980s were few and far between. At the time it was difficult to purchase a Routemaster direct from London Transport unless you lived outside the London area. Initially vehicles that were sold directly from London Transport included some of the former garage Showbuses (eg RMs 8, 254, 737, 1000, 1563 and 2116). Of these RM2116 is still preserved in its '1933' livery that it gained in 1983 as part of the celebrations to commemorate 50 years of London Transport.

As it's now 29 years since the main sales commenced from London Transport, many buses have had up to four or more owners. Happily every variant of Routemaster is represented in preservation.

Museum collections holding examples of Routemasters include the Cobham Bus Museum in Surrey with RML3 and RMC1461, Aston Manor Road Transport Museum in Birmingham with RM506, the Greater Manchester Museum with RM1414, the private Moseley Museum in West Yorkshire with RML2474, the Keighley Museum in West Yorkshire with RM736, and the Birmingham and Midland Museum of Transport (BaMMOT) at Wythall on the outskirts of Birmingham with RCL2219. All of these vehicles are actually owned by individuals, with the single exception of Greater Manchester's RM1414, which was donated by London Transport in January 1983. Ensign Bus at Purfleet in Essex have a collection of heritage vehicles that includes seven operational Routemasters, which are available for hire or are used on special services. They also own several other Routemasters that are in storage or being worked on in preparation for use.

Generally, when Routemasters are acquired for preservation they're returned to London red livery. Among these vehicles just about every example of London red livery is represented. However, many other liveries, including Strathtay Scottish and United Counties to name but two, have disappeared entirely and aren't represented in the ranks of preserved Routemasters. Among the few vehicles that have returned to their former non-London liveries are examples of the former red and yellow Clydeside Scottish, two-tone blue and yellow Kelvin Scottish, blue and white Southend Transport, and red and white Blackpool Transport.

RM2186 and RM2208 have been restored to 1979 Shillibeer livery and are the only surviving Routemasters that carried this. Three of the

BELOW A Routemaster still with a low-numbered body, RM14 was a well-known garage Showbus in the 1980s, but following an accident it was sold for scrap in 1994. It was rescued by its present owner in 2002 and has been made roadworthy, although a repaint is awaited.
(Mark Kehoe)

RCLs that have been fully restored, namely 2219, 2229 and 2233, have been restored in original Green Line livery, and of the six preserved RMCs five have been restored to original Lincoln green livery. The exception is RMC1476, which has received the 1970s National Bus Company leaf green scheme. So far ten RMLs have been returned to green livery, with most of them receiving Lincoln green and three receiving the later-style London Country livery from the National Bus Company era. RML2524 has retained its 2004 Shillibeer livery and RML2514 has been returned to maroon and cream Kentish Bus livery.

A reverse situation has occurred with RMs 541, and 759, which are currently preserved in liveries that Routemasters never actually carried

in passenger service: RM541 carries blue and ivory Samuel Ledgard livery, and former Strathtay Scottish RM759 carries white, green and orange Glasgow Corporation livery.

The former Northern General RMF fleet of 52 vehicles has declined drastically. Only four are preserved, including the original RMF1254, which was restored to original as-built London Transport condition for the Routemaster 50 celebrations in 2004. Two of the others have been restored to Northern maroon and cream colours.

Just over half of the former British Airways RMA class currently survives, but only a few are preserved. Two vehicles were restored to original mid-blue and white BEA livery but only one of these remains preserved, this being BEA1 (otherwise remembered as RMA28).

As has been mentioned elsewhere, several Routemasters have been rebuilt by owners after being cannibalised by bus companies and sold off for scrap. Another way of acquiring a Routemaster is to purchase one direct from a scrapyard and undertake a complete rebuild.

Today it has become common for vehicles to be preserved within bus companies, or by companies specialising in private hire work, weddings, corporate hire etc. As well as being a way to cover maintenance costs this has seen several successful companies formed, which has led in turn to the regular use of Routemasters in many parts of the United Kingdom.

Developed by London Transport in the 1950s to meet the tough operating conditions of the capital, the Routemaster bus became an icon in its own right. But it has now become even more than that. At an average age of nearly 50 years, and with over 1,200 examples surviving worldwide, the Routemaster has become *the* London bus, and the ultimate symbol of traditional London.

Appendix 1

A selection of notable surviving Routemasters

RM1

In April 1973, RM1 was sold to Lockheed Hydraulic Brake, but its use seems to have been very spasmodic and it was often seen parked in the famous 'dip' at London Transport's Chiswick Works. In 1980 it was reacquired by London Transport and was quickly dispatched to Aldenham Works to be restored as a display vehicle; it made its debut in May 1982 at the North Weald rally and was donated to London Transport Museum in March 1985. Twenty-five years later it remains with London Transport Museum and is often seen at various events in and around London.

RM2

After withdrawal RM2 was allocated to the Chiswick experimental department, where it remained often hidden from view until it appeared in two special liveries – silver in 1976 and dark green-based Shillibeer livery in 1978 – to promote HM the Queen's Silver Jubilee and the 150th anniversary of the Omnibus

respectively, and to attract potential advertisers for the vehicles to be used during these celebrations in 1977 and 1979, before returning to standard red livery in the latter year. During the early 1980s it became a regular attendee at rallies and was donated to London Transport Museum in March 1985. It remains with London Transport Museum, but early in the 21st century work commenced to rebuild its front to near original condition.

RM3

RM3 was withdrawn from training duties in 1972 and after a period of storage it was sold to the London Bus Preservation Group at Cobham in Surrey. In 2004, still with the

BELOW At every fifth anniversary, a commemorative run across London takes place in early February to celebrate the introduction of RM1 into passenger service. *(Mark Kehoe)*

FAR RIGHT RM2 has been seen at Acton Depot for several years in green undercoat, and gradually its new front panels are being fabricated. Its debut is eagerly awaited.
(Mark Kehoe)

same owners, it was rebuilt back to original style and was renumbered RML3 as part of the Routemaster 50 commemorations. Thus it became the first of the prototypes to be restored to original condition.

CRL4

In October 1966 RMC4 was transferred to Hatfield garage, where it remained almost without interruption until withdrawal in 1979. From this time onwards it was used for special events and was often seen on enthusiast runs to commemorate particular routes. However, to complete the story, RMC4 passed with the other London Country Routemasters to the newly formed London Country Bus Services Ltd on 1 January 1970 as part of the National Bus Company. By this time the Green Line network was being cut back and numerous RMCs, including RMC4, were from this time used on standard bus work.

RMC4 remained with London Country throughout the 1980s and passed to the Drawlane Group upon privatisation of the London Country South West subsidiary in February 1988. In December 1992 Drawlane was renamed British Bus and was acquired by the Cowie Group in June 1996. London Country South West had become London & Country from 1989, but in 1997 was rebranded as Arriva Serving Surrey & West Sussex. Throughout all these changes of ownership and company name RMC4 remained part of the same small vintage fleet. This was finally split up under Arriva ownership and RMC4 was sold for preservation in February 2000. In June 2007 it was acquired by the Kent-based London Bus Company.

RMF1254

RMF1254 was fitted with a Leyland 0600 engine before joining its sisters at Northern General in November 1966. It then operated around the Newcastle and Gateshead areas until sold in March 1981. It gradually lost some of its London features, including indicator ears, two-piece windscreen, radiator grille trim, wheel trim and some of its wind-down windows.

After many years in storage it was fully restored to original London condition, completed with an AEC engine and made its debut at the Routemaster 50 celebrations in July 2004. From

ABOVE RML3 was the first of the prototypes to be restored to original condition and is regularly seen out and about in connection with Cobham Bus Museum. *(Mark Kehoe)*

BELOW RMC4 now sees occasional use in passenger service at various events, but the long-term aim is to rebuild it back to original as-delivered condition. *(Mark Kehoe)*

ABOVE In October 2005 RMF1254 became technically the last Routemaster to enter service on a normal London route when it was used on the last day of crew operation on route 38. *(Mark Kehoe)*

ABOVE When serious fire damage has occurred to a Routemaster the vehicle usually has to be scrapped, but RM1368 survived and was the only Routemaster converted to single-deck by London Transport. *(Andrew Morgan)*

RIGHT BEA1 is one of the few former BEA/British Airways Routemasters to be actively preserved and a repaint is likely to be carried out soon. *(Mark Kehoe)*

time to time it can be seen at various events and private hires in the London area.

RM1368

At the end of 1973 RM1368 suffered fire damage at Tottenham garage, and in 1975 the damaged upper deck was removed and the vehicle was allocated to the experimental department at Chiswick Works as a single-decker. There it replaced RM8, which had been at Chiswick since it was built in 1958 and finally entered service for the first time in 1976. RM8 thus became the last Routemaster to enter passenger service.

RM1368 continued to see use at Chiswick Works until April 1989 and was involved in numerous trials, including the fitment of an LPG-powered engine in 1977, becoming possibly the first LPG-powered bus in the UK.

The next few years saw an uncertain future for this vehicle as it was vandalised and then passed through a number of dealers' hands, with the threat of possible export hanging over it. It was rescued by the author of this book in October 1997 and has been restored to its 1970s Chiswick Works condition.

BEA1

BEA1 remained in service with British European Airways (BEA) and then British Airways from October 1966 until April 1979. It then passed to London Transport as numerically the first of the

third and final batch to form the RMA class, and thus became RMA28, on paper at least.

However, it never entered service with its new owner and in November 1982 it was sold for preservation. In the summer of 1983 it made its debut superbly restored back to original condition complete with the illuminated panels. During the course of the subsequent 28 years it has passed through the hands of a number of owners and remains in preservation.

FRM1

The final production version of the Routemaster, FRM1 survived in service until February 1983, a total of almost 16 years. It spent its last seven years on the Round London Sightseeing Tours from Stockwell garage before being donated to the London Transport Museum in 1984, with whom it still sees occasional, albeit very limited, use.

RML2760

Numerically the last Routemaster to be delivered (in early February 1968), RML2760 went on to achieve 36 years in passenger service in London. The majority of this time was spent operating from Upton Park garage in East London. It was overhauled at Aldenham Works for the second time in 1982, by which time its status had been recognised and it regained its original body, B2760. It was withdrawn in June 2004 when route 8 lost its Routemasters and has subsequently led a sheltered life, its use being quite rare because of the introduction of the London Low Emission Zone.

Appendix 2

How many roadworthy Routemasters survive worldwide?

Below is a list of all known surviving Routemasters as at the time of writing:

UK

AEC-engined	
RM	126
RMF	4
RMC	16
RCL	15
RML	6
BEA (RMA)	18
FRM	1
Total	186 (27.4% of the overall total)
Leyland-engined	
RML	1
RM	26
RMC	1
RMF	5
Total	33 (4.9% of the overall total)
Iveco-engined	
RM	9
RMC	1
RML	70
Total	80 (11.8% of the overall total)
Cummins C-series	
RM	2
RMC	1
RCL	1
RML	195
Total	199 (29.3% of the overall total)
Cummins B-series	
RM	59 (includes the ERMs)
RMC	1
RCL	2
RML	26
BEA (RMA)	4
Total	92 (13.5% of the overall total)
Cummins ISBe	
RM	1 (0.15% of the overall total)
Scania DS9	
RM	52
RML	28
Total	80 (11.8% of the overall total)
DAF DK1160VS-engined	
RM	1 (0.15% of the overall total)
LPG-engined	
RM	1 (0.15% of the overall total)
Un-engined	
RM	2
RML	5
Total	7 (1.0% of the overall total)
Total number of Routemasters in the UK: 680.	

Notes

All Routemasters are fitted with the standard D182 gearbox, except those fitted with the Euro II Cummins B-series engine or the Euro III Cummins ISBe engine, which now have Allison gearboxes fitted. However, out of those fitted with Cummins B-series engines 38 are fitted with the Allison MT643 gearbox and 54 are fitted with the Allison T270 gearbox.

Eight Routemasters (five RMs and three RMLs) fitted with Cummins B-series engines are also fitted with a Telma Axial Retarder, model reference AC50-80.

The single RM fitted with the Cummins ISBe engine, RM1562, is also fitted with an Allison T270 gearbox and a Telma retarder.

One RML has been fitted with a Cummins C-series engine but has also been fitted with a ZF 4HP400 gearbox with integral retarder.

Outside the UK

Exact details of Routemasters overseas are sketchy at best, with details of some countries being better than others. Some vehicles haven't been reported for many years, but it isn't unusual for vehicles to suddenly reappear many years after being exported. Consequently the totals below are for all Routemasters reported overseas, with the only omissions being those confirmed as having been scrapped.

RM	407
RML	161
RMC	12
RCL	5
RMF	5
BEA (RMA)	10
Total	600

The approximate total number of surviving Routemasters worldwide is therefore 1,280, out of a total number of 2,876 built.

Appendix 3

Routemaster types

Bodywork

Park Royal, or LTE/PRV (RM1 and 2), or Weymann (RM3), or Eastern Coach Works (RMC4).

Years built

RM	1954, 1955, 1957–65
RMA	1966–67
RMC	1957, 1962
RMF	1964–65
RML	1961–62, 1965–68
RCL	1965
FRM	1966

Numbers built

RM	2,123
RMA	65
RMC	69
RMF	51
RML	524
RCL	43
FRM	1
Total	2,876

Subframes

AEC Routemaster model	R2RH	All RM/RMC vehicles
	R2RH/1	RML2261–2760
	R2RH/3	RCL2218–2260
	R2RH/2	RMA1–65
	2R2RH	All RM vehicles originally fitted with Leyland units
	3R2RH	RMF1254 and former Northern General vehicles
	FR2R	FRM

Engine types

AEC AV590	120mm bore x 142mm stroke with a capacity of 9.65 litres (588in^3) and developing 115bhp at 1,800rpm.
AEC AV690	130mm bore x 142mm stroke with a capacity of 11.3 litres (690in^3) and developing 175bhp at 2,200rpm.
AEC AV691	11.3 litres, developing 150bhp at 1,800rpm.
Cummins C-series	114mm bore x 135mm stroke with a capacity of 8.27 litres (504.5in^3) and developing 150bhp at 2,200rpm.
Cummins B-series	102mm bore x 120mm stroke with a capacity of 5.9 litres (360in^3) and developing 145bhp at 2,500rpm.
Cummins ISBe series	5.9 litres, developing 185bhp at 2,500rpm.
DAF DK1160VS	11.6 litres, rated at 145bhp at 1,800rpm.
Iveco 836/1	115mm bore x 130mm stroke with a capacity of 8.102 litres (494in^3) and developing 130bhp at 1,850rpm.
Leyland 0600	121.92mm bore x 139.70mm stroke with a capacity of 9.78 litres (597in^3) and developing 115bhp at 1,800rpm.
Scania DS9	115mm bore x 144mm stroke with a capacity of 9.0 litres (549in^3) and developing 150bhp at 2,200rpm.

Appendix 4

Routemaster codes

Body codes

Standard bus body codes are as follows:

Body type	Highbridge double-deck bus	H
	Open-top double-deck bus	O
Seating capacity	The upper-deck seating capacity is shown first, followed by the total for the lower deck	
Entrance position	Front entrance with platform doors	F
	Rear entrance without doors	R
	Rear entrance with doors	RD

These codes are used to describe bus body types, seating capacity and entrance position, in that order. Therefore a standard 64-seat Routemaster's code would be 'H36/28R', which would signify 36 seats upstairs and 28 seats downstairs.

Class codes

These abbreviations were used to identify the various models of Routemaster, as follows:

RM   Standard Routemaster.
RMA   Front-entrance Routemaster (ex-BEA/ British Airways).
RMC   Routemaster coach (ex-Green Line).
RML   Routemaster lengthened.
RMF   Front-entrance Routemaster lengthened (ex-Northern General).
RME   Routemaster extended (former RMA).
RCL   Routemaster coach lengthened (ex-Green Line).
ER   Extended Routemaster (RML).
ERM   Extended open-top Routemaster (RM).
DRM   RML fitted with RMC rear end including platform doors.
FRM   Front-entrance Routemaster (rear engine), originally to be classified as RMR.

Chassis and body classification codes

Originally London Transport applied codes to all Routemasters, with stamped brass plates being riveted to the bodywork on the nearside of the drivers' cab below the front of the emergency window. The system fell out of use in the 1980s but vehicles should all retain these plates.

The first brass plate indicated the body code, eg 'RM 5/2', and the second plate the chassis and body code, eg '2/5 RM 5/2'. On the latter plate, the prefix number(s) shows the chassis modification level, with the digit nearest to the 'RM' denoting the more significant changes, while any digit before the '/' indicated a sub-group. The 'RM' letters denote the Routemaster family. The suffix number(s) shows the body variant, again with the digit nearest to the 'RM' being more significant.

The various sub-groups indicated various configurations, including the alternator system fitted, transmission type (CAV or SCG), brake system (Lockheed or Clayton), offside illuminated advert fitted, and individual Routemaster type (eg RM or RCL etc). The base codes were as follows:

1RM1   for the prototype RM1.
2RM2   for the prototype RM2.
3RM3   for the prototype RM3.
4RM4   for the prototype RM4.
5RM5   for the standard production Routemaster.
6RM6   for the RMC production batch.
7RM7   for the RML class.
7RM8   for the forward-entrance RMF1254.
8RM10   for the RCL class.
9RM9   as for the 5RM5, but with offside illuminated advert panels.
9RM12   for the BEA Routemasters.
10RM11 for the sole FRM.

Engine numbers/codes

London Transport used its own reference numbers for each engine type and variation, and some older engines will still have plates or tags bearing these numbers. Those for the Routemaster are as follows:

EN45   AEC AV590 (early type with thick lead bronze bearings).
EN52   Leyland 0600.
EN54   AEC AV590 (later type with thin reticular tin bearings).
EN55   AEC AV690 (fitted originally to RMs but subsequently converted to standard as 9.6-litre AV590).
EN60   AEC AV690 (as fitted to RCLs rated at 115bhp at 1,800rpm).
EN61   AEC AV690 (as fitted to BEA coaches rated at 175bhp at 2,200rpm).
EN62   AEC AV590 (later type with thin reticular tin bearings and DPA fuel pump; these were originally fitted to the last batch of RMLs, but later to many RMs as well).

There were also many variations to the standard AEC AV590 engine within the 'EN' engine codes above. Subsequent engine types fitted to the Routemaster from other manufacturers and suppliers did not receive London Transport engine reference numbers.

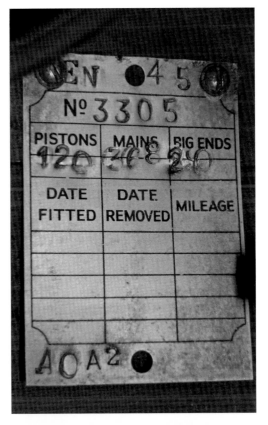

LEFT Original style plates, as fitted to an AEC AV590 engine by London Transport, can still be found on some engines. As well as the unit serial number, the code numbers signify the main and big-end bearing sizes fitted, and the date the engine was last overhauled. *(Andrew Morgan)*

RIGHT Two numbers can clearly be seen on the front nearside of this A-frame. The number stamped on the brass plate signifies that this is A-frame A1881, and the number stamped on the side of the A-frame is 2R2RH1863 which, when new, was originally fitted to RM1867. The 2R2RH, rather than the earlier R2RH reference, signifies that this subframe was fitted with a Leyland engine when new. *(Mark Kehoe)*

Appendix 5

Glossary of terms and abbreviations

These are some of the terms used within this book, many of which are unique to the Routemaster or London buses of the period in general and may require some explanation.

Accumulators – Pressure storage reservoirs for front and rear wheel braking. Once the accumulators have been charged to the correct pre-charge pressure (500–550psi) they maintain a continuous-flow circuit. The hydraulic pump is mounted to the front of the gearbox (except on Cummins B-series re-engined vehicles, which have an engine-mounted pump). It pumps filtered hydraulic oil from the offside mounted header tank direct to the two accumulators and increases the pressure to a cut-out level of 1,200–1,250psi. In the event of pump failure several brake applications can still be made to bring the bus safely to rest. The accumulator itself is a container that's divided into two chambers by means of a sliding piston or a rubber bladder. An air pre-charge is applied to one chamber, and when the pump is running oil is forced into the other chamber and further compresses the air. The Routemaster was originally fitted with two types of accumulator, manufactured by either Lockheed or Clayton. The Lockheed type are cylindrical, torpedo-like steel tubes with caps on each end, whereas the now rare Clayton type are spherical steel balls fitted with a rubber bladder.

ACV – Associated Commercial Vehicles Limited. See AEC entry.

AEC – The shortened title of the Associated Equipment Company. Formed in 1912, it was originally based in Walthamstow in East London before moving to Southall in West London in 1927. AEC became known as a leading builder of commercial vehicle chassis and diesel engines used all around the world. It was particularly famous as the 'Builder of London's Buses'. In 1948, with the acquisition and merging of further businesses, Associated Commercial Vehicles Limited (ACV) was formed as the parent company, with AEC as one of it manufacturing subsidiaries. ACV was acquired by Leyland Motors Limited in 1962 and followed it into nationalisation as part of British Leyland (BL), with the Southall plant being closed in 1979 as the BL empire struggled to survive.

Aldenham Works – Officially opened in 1956 and became the main London Transport bus overhaul works. It was located near Elstree in Hertfordshire, to the north-west of London.

The site was originally developed for the Underground Northern Line extension to Bushey Heath, as part of the 1930s New Works Programme, and was to have become the main Northern Line depot. Although almost complete at the outbreak of World War Two, the railway extension works were stopped and never completed. During the war the site was used as an aircraft factory, producing Handley Page Halifax bombers as part of the London Aircraft Production consortium. After the war the Northern Line extension plan was abandoned and the site was converted to a new role as Aldenham Bus Overhaul Works. At its peak around 50 buses were overhauled per week and it became an industrial-scale operation. All bodywork overhauls, repaints and major repairs were carried out at Aldenham, while the mechanical units were dealt with separately at London Transport's Chiswick Works. After various cost-cutting attempts throughout the early 1980s the works were closed in November 1986 and the site was cleared and demolished in 1996.

A-frame – The name given to the front subframe that carries the engine, steering and pedal gear. It's attached to the body adjacent to the second main body crossmember and at the lower front bulkhead mounting. The subframes were also known as 'wheel-barrows'.

B-frame – The name given to the rear subframe, rear suspension unit or 'bogie', which carries the rear axle and rear suspension. At the rear of the subframe are located the coil spring suspension (or the self-levelling air-bellows, as originally fitted to the RMA, RMC and RCL vehicles). The rear axle tube passes through the radius arms and is located by bonded rubber 'sandwich' mountings on each side. The front of the side frames, or radius arms, are attached to the third main body bearer.

BEA – British European Airways existed from 1946 until 1974. The airline operated European and North African routes from airports around the United Kingdom. BEA ceased operations in 1974, when it was merged with the British Overseas Airways Corporation (BOAC) to form British Airways.

Boat – A box member of welded construction bolted to the outside of the front subframe members, to the top and bottom ends of which are attached the wishbone assemblies.

Chiswick Works – Opened in 1921 by the London General Omnibus Company (LGOC) as a central workshop for the repair, overhaul and construction of buses, parts and equipment on a single site, with the intention of reducing costs and improving efficiency. The works covered a 32-acre site just off Chiswick High Road in West London. Also based there was the driver and conductor training school with its infamous skid patch. The production of bus bodywork was undertaken from the mid-1920s to the early 1940s, ending with the first batch of RTs. With the general cost-cutting that took place in the 1980s, the adoption of competitive tendering and the setting up of separate bus operating companies, Chiswick Works was found to be surplus to requirements and was finally closed down in 1990.

Dustbin lids – The colloquial name given to the rear-wheel disc covers that were fitted to some London buses up until late 1971.

Ears – The colloquial name given to the original type of front indicators fitted to the Routemaster, which are located on swivel brackets on the relief band. The indicator bulb is located inside a black rubber housing with orange-coloured lenses. These black rubber housings stick out from the vehicle and were known as 'elephant ears', whence the abbreviated name 'ears'.

EP – Electro-pneumatic.

Fibreshield – The trade name used by Transmatic Europe Limited, who supplied London Buses with domes to fit over the existing aluminium front roof dome during the RML fleet refurbishment programme in the early 1990s. Known as 'Defender' domes by Transmatic and utilising the Fibreshield 4000 grade, they were manufactured in the USA from match-moulded composite to be flexible and damage-resistant. It's believed that copies have been subsequently manufactured, but these are of a different and less flexible material.

IM – Integrally mounted (*ie* chassisless).

Intensifier – Also known as the K-9, after the infamous *Doctor Who* robot dog, this is used to charge the accumulators with air. London Transport used the bus garage compressor-fed (moisture-free) air supply to charge accumulators, with the required pressure being generated by a differential-piston pump or 'intensifier'. An intensifier can be used with a workshop compressor of sufficient size. In the absence of an intensifier, accumulators can be charged instead using commercially available bottled nitrogen, which has the benefits of being clean and dry; suitable regulator and pressure gauges should be fitted and similar procedures should then be followed.

Leyland Motors – Beginning in 1896, Leyland has a long history of manufacturing commercial vehicles, lorries and buses. In 1962 Leyland Motors acquired Associated Commercial Vehicles (ACV), including AEC (see above) and Park Royal Vehicles (see below), and was renamed Leyland Motor Corporation. In 1968 it was merged with British Motor Holdings (BMH) to form the British Leyland Motor Corporation (BLMC). With this merger, the new organisation included Daimler, Guy, BMC, Land Rover, Rover, MG, Triumph, Austin and Morris. In 1975, following publication of the Ryder Report, BLMC was effectively nationalised as British Leyland (BL), with the British Government as its major shareholder. The new company was restructured and split into four divisions including Leyland Truck and Bus, which took control of truck and bus production. This division was further split into Leyland Trucks and Leyland Bus in 1981. The bus operation was sold in 1986 as a management buy-out to form Leyland Bus, and was subsequently bought by Volvo Buses in 1988. Unlike Leyland Bus, Leyland Trucks survived and has passed through a number of owners to become part of US truck manufacturer PACCAR.

LOTS – London Omnibus Traction Society.

Moquette – A versatile and hard-wearing material, predominantly wool with a small percentage of polyester, which is used to cover the Routemaster's passenger seats. The fabric is still woven in Yorkshire, using traditional techniques that are required to match exacting standards. Moquette continues to be renowned for its highly durable and fire-resistant qualities.

Park Royal Vehicles – Based in London NW10, this became a sister company to AEC within the Associated Commercial Vehicles group (ACV). The origins of coachbuilding at Park Royal can be traced back to 1924, before a new company was established in 1930 that then became Park Royal Vehicles (PRV) in 1946. In 1949 it was acquired by ACV, after which its history mirrored that of AEC until closure of the plant in 1980, a year later than AEC.

PCV – Passenger-carrying vehicle.

PSV – Public service vehicle.

PVR – Peak vehicle requirement.

RMOOA – The Routemaster Operators & Owners Association, more often referred to simply as the Routemaster Association.

RPC – Reduced pollution certificate.

SSG – Speed sensitive generator.

Transmatic lighting – Modular fluorescent lighting system from Transmatic Europe Ltd that enhanced lighting levels without increasing the power required. Experimentally fitted in 1988 and subsequently saw widespread use in the RML fleet during the early 1990s refurbishment programme, as well as amongst numerous Routemaster fleets outside London, including Clydeside Scottish and Southend Transport. A fluorescent lighting conversion kit was also fitted to destination indicator displays as part of the RML refurbishment programme; these were also supplied by Transmatic Europe Ltd.

Treadmaster – Resilient, rubber-bonded cork flooring specifically designed for the transport industry. A very safe, slip-resistant material even in wet conditions, it also demonstrates exceptional wear-resistance and absorbs sound.

Appendix 6

Useful contacts

Absolute Charters Inc (trading as
Ambassatours Gray Line Tours)
2631 King Street, Halifax
Nova Scotia B3K 4T7
Canada
Website www.ambassatours.com
Also at St John, New Brunswick,
Canada

Arriva London
16 Watsons Road
London N22 7TZ
Tel 020 8271 0101
Website www.arrivalondon.com/
thearrivaheritagefleet

Aston Manor Road Transport Museum
208–216 Witton Lane
Birmingham B6 6QE
Website www.amrtm.org

The Brake House
Unit 7
Imex House
6 Wadsworth Road
Greenford
Middlesex UB6 7JJ
Tel 020 8998 4009
Fax 020 8998 0510
Specialists in the relining of brake shoes
and drums.

The BusWorks (Totally Transport CIC)
South Shore Business Park
off Burton Road
Blackpool FY4 4NW
Tel 01253 699039
Website www.thebusworks.co.uk
Specialists in restoration and
refurbishment of classic and modern

buses.
Carlyle Bus & Coach Limited
Carlyle Business Park
Great Bridge Street
Swan Village
West Bromwich B70 0XA
Tel 0121 524 1200
Fax 0121 524 1201
Website www.carlyleplc.co.uk
A leading supplier of parts for the
bus and coach industry worldwide,
including Treadmaster flooring.

Cobham Bus Museum
The London Bus Preservation Trust Ltd
Cobham Hall
Brooklands Road, Weybridge
Surrey KT13 0QN
Website www.lbpt.org

C.O.H. Baines Limited
Unit 3,
Buckingham House
Longfield Road, Tunbridge Wells
Kent TN2 3EY
Tel 01892 543311
Website www.coh-baines.co.uk
Stockists of rubber extrusions and
mouldings, including some to suit the
Routemaster.

Dinex Exhaust Limited
14 Chesford Grange
Woolston
Warrington
Cheshire WA1 4RE
Tel 01925 849849
Fax 01925 849850
Website www.dinexexhausts.com
Exhaust system manufacturer and
supplier in UK and Europe, usually via

agents such as Partco.
Dreadnought Coaches
198 Allerburn Lea, Alnwick
Northumberland NE66 2QR
Tel 01665 603022
Website
www.dreadnoughtcoaches.co.uk

Ensign Bus
Juliette Close
Purfleet Industrial Park, Purfleet
Essex RM15 4YF
Tel 01708-865656
Website www.ensignbus.com

The Ghost Bus Tours Ltd
33 New Oxford Street
London WC1A 1BH
Tel 0844 5678 666
Website www.theghostbustours.com

Go Ahead London
18 Merton High Street
London SW19 1DN
Tel 020 8545 6100
Website www.go-ahead-london.com

Greater Manchester Museum of
Transport
Boyle Street, Cheetham Hill
Manchester M8 8UW
Website www.gmts.co.uk

Holdsworth Fabrics Limited
Hopton Mills, Mirfield
West Yorkshire WF14 8HE
Tel 01924 490591
Fax 01924 495605
Website www.camirafabrics.com
Supplier of seating moquette; along with
Interface Fabrics and British Furtex Fabrics

Ltd they are now part of the Camira Group.
Imperial Engineering Limited
Delamere Road, Cheshunt
Hertfordshire EN8 9UD
Tel 01992 634255
Fax 01992 630506
Website www.imperialengineering.co.uk
Suppliers and remanufacturers of
steering, braking, hydraulic and
mechanical components.

Keighley Museum
c/o 47 Brantfell Drive
Burnley, Lancashire BB12 8AW
Tel 01282 413179
Website www.kbmt.org.uk

Local Haunts LLP
Gallery Zero One
53 Albert Road, Southsea
Hampshire PO5 2SF
Tel 0800 389 6897
Website www.localhaunts.com

London Bus and Truck Limited
Units 1–4, Northfleet Industrial Estate
Lower Road, Northfleet
Kent DA11 9SN
Tel 01474 361199
Fax 01474 361188
Website www.londonbusandtruck.co.uk
Specialists in bodywork repair,
restoration and repainting, as well as
some mechanical work.

London Bus Company Ltd
Units 1–4 Northfleet Industrial Estate
Lower Road, Northfleet
Kent DA11 9SN
Tel 01474 361199
Website www.thelondonbuscompany.
co.uk

London Omnibus Engineering Services
24 Chaldon Way
Coulsdon
Surrey CR5 1DB
Tel/fax 01737 552276
Website http://freespace.virgin.net/
lionel.moss/loes.htm
For parts, technical assistance and

worldwide on-site help.
London Transport Museum
Covent Garden Piazza
London WC2E 7BB
Tel 0 20 7379 6344; *Fax* 020 7565 7254
Website www.ltmuseum.co.uk
Collection includes a wide range
of materials and media, including
vehicles, posters, signs, uniforms,
photographs, ephemera, maps and
engineering drawings, claimed to be
the most comprehensive record of
urban mass transit in the world. It has
five Routemasters, including RM1,
RM2 and the unique front-entrance
rear-engined FRM1. Only RM1737 is
on display at Covent Garden.

London Transport Museum Depot
2 Museum Way
118–120 Gunnersbury Lane
London W3 9BQ
Website www.ltmuseum.co.uk/whats-
on/museum-depot/events
Holds the majority of the London
Transport Museum's collections that aren't
on display in the main museum in Covent
Garden. Opens to the public for special
events, including themed open weekends.

Mac Tours
c/o Lothian Buses plc
Annandale Street, Edinburgh EH7 4AZ
Tel 0131 554 4494
Website www.edinburghtour.com/en/
our-tours-g/mac-tours-vintage-bus-live-
guide.html
or
Edinburgh Bus Tours
Waverley Bridge, Edinburgh EH1 1BQ
Tel 0131 220 0770

McKenna Brothers Limited
McKenna House, Jubilee Road
Middleton, Manchester M24 2LX
Tel 0161 655 3244
Fax 0161 655 3059
Website www.mckennabrothers.co.uk
A supplier of destination blinds in the
UK and worldwide, including authentic
reproduction blinds to suit preserved or

heritage vehicles.
Mitchell Diesel Limited
Fulwood Road South
Fulwood Industrial Estate
Sutton-in-Ashfield
Nottinghamshire NG17 2JZ
Tel 01623 550550
Fax 01623 443041
Website www.mitchells.co.uk
Mitchell Powersystems are the sole
UK and Ireland distributor for Allison
Transmission, and also hold extensive
parts stock and provide service support.

Premium Tours Ltd
Suite 14, 232 Copenhagen Street
London N1 0AW
Tel 0207 713 1311
Website www.premiumtours.co.uk

PVS Barnsley Limited
Boulder Bridge Lane, off Shaw Lane
Carlton, Barnsley, South Yorkshire
Tel 01226 722052
Fax 01226 700261
Website www.pvsbuses.com
Specialist in the dismantling of
redundant buses, sadly including many
Routemasters; they've also salvaged
many parts for the benefit of vehicle
owners and are able to export engine
units and axles etc.

Queensbridge PSV Limited
Milner Way, Longlands Industrial Estate
Ossett, West Yorkshire WF5 9JE
Tel 01924 281871
Fax 01924 281807
Website www.queensbridgeltd.co.uk
Remanufacturers of gearbox and
transmission units.

Rigton Insurance Services Limited
Chevin House, Otley Road, Guiseley,
Leeds, West Yorkshire LS20 8BH
Tel 01943-879539
Fax 01943-875529
Website www.rigtoninsurance.co.uk
Specialist insurance brokers, in
partnership with Chaucer Insurance, for
preserved vehicles, including optional

breakdown cover.

Routemaster Association
c/o 31 Pooley Avenue
Egham
Surrey TW20 8AD
Website www.routemaster.co.uk
The Routemaster Association is the sole dedicated organisation for operators and owners of Routemaster vehicles. Its principal aims are to share knowledge and operating experience, to provide technical information, help with obtaining spare parts and Routemaster-related news, and to cater for historical and preservation interests. The Association is also a supplier and stockist of some specialist parts including, Treadmaster flooring and Routemaster window rubbers. Graham Lunn is the association secretary at the time of writing.

Scottish Travel
c/o Wilson's Coaches
15 Dellingburn Street
Greenock
Strathclyde PA15 4TW
Tel 01475 781957
Website www.glasgowcitytour.com

South Devon Railway
The Station
Buckfastleigh
Devon TQ11 0DZ
Tel 0845 345 1420
Website www.southdevonrailway.co.uk

Sullivan Buses
Sullivan Bus & Coach Ltd
First Floor
Deards House
St Albans Road
South Mimms Service Area
Potters Bar
Hertfordshire EN6 3NE
Tel 01707 646803
Website www.sullivanbuses.co.uk

Timebus Travel
Boleyn Drive, St Albans
Hertfordshire AL1 2BP
Tel 01727 866248
Website www.timebus.co.uk

Towergate Risk Solutions (Towergate Underwriting Group Limited)
Adams Tingle House
Kettering Parkway West, Kettering
Northamptonshire NN15 6XW
Tel 01536 486700
Fax 01536 486786
Website
www.towergaterisksolutions.co.uk
Specialist insurance brokers for preserved vehicles in exhibition use or passenger-carrying, including optional full UK roadside assistance.

The Transport Museum
Chapel Lane
Wythall
Worcestershire B47 6JX
Tel 01564 826471
Website www.bammot.org.uk

Ward Jones Commercial Vehicles Limited
Binders Industrial Estate
Cryers Hill Road, Cryers Hill
High Wycombe
Buckinghamshire HP15 6LJ
Tel 01494 711510
Fax 01494 711297
Specialists in the maintenance, servicing and repair of commercial vehicles, including Routemasters.

Western Greyhound
Western House
St Austell Street, Summercourt
Near Newquay
Cornwall TR8 5DDR
Tel 01637 871871
Website www.westerngreyhound.com

Woolies (I. & C. Woolstenholmes Limited)
Whitley Way
Northfields Industrial Estate
Market Deeping
Peterborough
Cambridgeshire PE6 8AR
Tel 01778 347347
Fax 01778 341847
Website www.woolies-trim.co.uk
Suppliers of trim, upholstery and fittings, including some rubber extrusions and mouldings to suit the Routemaster.

Finally, there are the two Heritage routes, which must count as one of London's best-kept secrets. They're operated by First London (website www.firstgroup.com/ukbus/greater_london) and Stagecoach London (website www.stagecoachbus.com/default.aspx?Operator=London&Location=London) under contract to Transport *for* London (TfL). Further details can theoretically be obtained by contacting TfL:

TfL London Buses
4th floor
Zone Y4
14 Pier Walk
London SE10 0ES
Website www.tfl.gov.uk

– to whom the operating companies will normally direct you. Inexplicably, however, there's no direct information available at the time of writing on the TfL website concerning either of the Heritage routes! Some details of these operations are provided in Chapter 5 ('The Routemaster in the 21st century'). Travel information for all of London's buses is available by telephoning 0843 222 1234.

Appendix 7

Further reading

Many dozens of books have been written about Routemasters, especially during the period when the last Routemasters were withdrawn from London service between 2003 and 2006, and the titles listed here represent only the most widely recognised key publications. The books published by Capital Transport and those written by Geoff Rixon are highly recommended and are a must for the dedicated Routemaster enthusiast; the standard of production and quality of the photographs in these is generally extremely high.

Baker, M.H.C. *The Routemaster* (Ian Allan, 2010).
Blacker, K. *Routemaster: Volume 1 1954–1969* (Capital Transport, 1991).
—— *Routemaster: Volume 2 1970–2005* (Capital Transport, 2007).
Blake, J. *Routemaster Reflections – 30 years of the Routemaster* (The Regent Press, 1984).
—— and Williamson, R. *Routemaster Roundabout – A Silver Jubilee of Service 1956–81* (Regent Transport Publishing, 1981).
Brown, S. *Bus Monograph 3: Routemaster* (Ian Allan, 1984).
Capital Transport. *London Transport's Silver Jubilee Buses* (Capital Transport, 1977).
Clark, R. *In Shades of Green* (Regent Transport Publishing, 1980).
Curtis, C. *The Routemaster Bus* (Midas Books, 1981).
—— *The Development of the Routemaster* (RMOOA, 1999).
Donaldson, G. *The Routemaster Years in Croydon & District* (Graydon Transport Publishing, 1994).
Elborough, T. *The Bus We Loved – London's Affair with the Routemaster* (Granta Books, 2005).
Fennell, S. *Routemasters Around Great Britain* (DPR Marketing & Sales, 1988).
Gascoine, P. *The London 'Advert Bus'* (P. Gascoine, 1977).
Godson, D. *Replacing the Routemaster* (Policy Exchange, 2005).
Jenkinson, K.A. *The Routemaster Outside London* (Autobus Review Publications, 1987).
—— *Routemaster Dispersal* 2nd Edition (Autobus Review Publications, 2000).
Morgan, A. *Routemaster 1954–1994: Celebrating the First Forty Years* (RMOOA/LTM, 1994).
—— *Routemaster Handbook* 3rd Edition (Capital Transport, 2001).
—— *Routemasters in Great Britain* 3rd Edition (LOTS, 2003).
—— *Working with Routemasters* (Capital Transport, 2004).
—— *Handbook for the Routemaster* (RMOOA, reprint with minor amendments, 2005).
—— and Lloyd, C. *Routemasters in London* 2nd Edition (LOTS, 1995).
—— and Watson, G. *Monarch of the Road – A Celebration of a London Icon* (RMOOA, 2007).
Obergfell, R. *Last Stop (Routemasters)* (Ralf Obergfell, 2008).
Rixon, G. *The Heyday of the Routemaster* (Ian Allan, 1997).
—— *Routemasters in Colour* (Ian Allan, 1999).
—— *Routemaster Jubilee* (Ian Allan, 2004).
—— and Fennell, S. *Bus Portfolio No 1: Routemaster* (DPR Marketing & Sales, 1987).

Robbs, S. *London's Routemaster – Garage Allocations (1956–2005)* (Stuart Robbs Publishing, 2008).
—— *London's Green Routemaster – Garage Allocations (1957–1980)* (Stuart Robbs Publishing, 2009).
Townsin, A. *Bus Profile – Routemaster* (Ian Allan, 1990).
Wagstaff, J. *The London 'Routemaster' Bus* (Oakwood Press, 1975).
Walker, G. *The New Routemaster Maintenance Manual* (Cream Band, 1995).
Ware, L. and P. *The Classic Routemaster Bus Illustrated* (Warehouse Publications, 1998).
Watson, G. *Rodney the Routemaster* (Clydeside, 1986).
Wharmby, M., and Rixon, G. *Routemaster Requiem* (Ian Allan, 2006).
—— *Routemaster Retrospective* (Ian Allan, 2007).
—— *Routemaster Omnibus* (Ian Allan, 2008).
Whiting, J. *The Birth of the Routemaster* (Capital Transport, 2004).
—— *London's Last Routemasters* (Capital Transport, 2006).
Willis, J.M. *Routemaster – The Last Eleven Months* (John Willis, 2006).

Some maintenance manuals can also be obtained:

London Transport Maintenance Bulletin No 47 (London Transport, 1961, and subsequent updated versions – out of print)
New Routemaster Maintenance Manual (C. & G. Walker, 1995).
Operator's Manual AT, MT, HT Series (Allison Transmission, 2001).
Mechanic's Tips MT (B) 600 Series (Allison Transmission, 1997).
Operator's Manual T Series (Allison Transmission, updated to 2010).
Cummins Parts Catalogue – 6CF, 6CT, 6CTA8.3.
Operation and Maintenance Manual C Series Diesel Engines (Cummins Engine Company Ltd).
Operation and Maintenance Manual Automotive, Recreational Vehicle and Bus B Series Engines (Cummins Engine Company Ltd).
Workshop Manual – 8361 Industrial (Iveco, 1980s).
Operator's Manual D9, DC9, DI9 Industrial engine (Scania Industrial & Marine Engines, 2001).
Work Description – 9-series engines (Scania Industrial & Marine Engines, 1997).
Compendium of Technical Articles and Handy Hints –
Part 1 (Newsletters 1–20) 2nd Edition (Routemaster Association, 1998).
Part 2 (Newsletters 21–40) (Routemaster Association, 2003).
Part 3 (Newsletters 41–60) (Routemaster Association, 2006).

The *London Transport Maintenance Bulletin No 47* of 1961 was the original maintenance manual for the Routemaster. C. & G. Walker's updated version of 1995 contains information on the AEC and Leyland engines, as well as sections on the mechanicals, bodywork and electrics. It also includes additional information on the Iveco engine.

Index

Advertising panels 20, 24, 28, 30, 35, 91, 94-95, 138, 153
AEC 10-13, 15, 17, 20-22, 92, 107, 145, 148
  RF (Regal IV) 16, 24, 28, 53
  RT bus (Regent III) 7, 9-12, 16, 21-22, 29, 32, 43, 53, 78-79, 137
Air system (compressor) 11, 14, 16, 19, 58-59, 112, 114, 124
Aldenham Works 10, 18, 22, 25-28, 31-35, 37-38, 82, 95, 97, 148, 150, 153
  works float 26-27
Annual servicing 108, 111, 114, 118, 120
Arriva 39-41, 43-45, 151
Authenticity 90-95
Axles 10, 60-61, 94, 121

Badges 18-19, 23, 92, 128, 148
Batteries 68-69, 88, 91, 112, 114, 126
Battery compartment 66, 77, 83, 91, 114, 128
Big Bus 39
Bodies 7, 11-13, 15-17, 19, 25-27, 35, 45, 47, 72-83, 95, 97, 114, 155
  codes and plates 72, 98, 156
  exchanges 25-27, 90
  inspection and lubrication 126-127
  numbers 27, 95, 147, 148
Bonnet 14-16, 18-19, 79-80, 114, 127
Braking system 7, 10-12, 15, 19-20, 23-24, 29, 47, 59, 62-66, 71, 87, 89, 92, 103, 105, 107, 112, 117, 119, 121-124, 141
  recharging 122-123
British European Airways (BEA)/ British Airways 23-25, 32, 37, 78, 90, 103, 135, 148, 152
BTS Coaches 40
Bus Electronic Scanning Indicator 28
Bus Engineering Ltd 32, 37

Chiswick Works 11-14, 18, 25, 32, 37, 97, 150, 152
Chobham Proving Ground 13
Chrome trim 91
Class designations 155-156
  CRL 15
  ERM 38, 41, 133-134
  FRM 24, 137, 146, 153
  RCL 16, 22-23, 25-26, 29, 31-34, 37-39, 41, 56, 61, 69, 90, 92, 103, 121, 134, 137, 142, 146
  RM 15, 20, 22, 29-30, 38-42, 89, 92, 96, 103, 121, 125, 127, 134-141, 146, 148, 152
  RMA (BEA) 16, 25-26, 32, 37, 39, 61, 69, 72, 78, 103, 121, 135, 141, 148, 152-153
  RMC 16-17, 22, 29, 32-33, 38, 41, 61, 69, 90, 96, 103, 121, 137, 140-142, 148
  RMF 23, 34, 39, 56, 103, 121, 148, 151
  RML (ER) 15, 19-20, 22-23, 25-26, 29-31, 33, 35, 39, 41-44, 56, 69, 80-81, 88-90, 92-93, 96, 103, 121, 127, 135, 137-138, 141-143, 153
  SRM 31
Cleaning 114

Cobham Bus Museum 137, 143, 146-147, 150-151
Colour schemes and liveries 28, 32, 35-36, 38-39, 82-83, 90, 92-94, 133, 138-143, 148
  all-over advertising 29-30, 35, 38
  gold 31, 41, 44
  green 14-17, 21, 23, 32, 133, 137, 141-142, 148
  interior 11, 14-15, 22, 42
  red 21, 25, 28, 30, 34, 40, 93, 102, 134, 138-140, 147, 150
  relief bands 16, 21, 23-25, 27-29, 93, 139, 142-143
  roundels, lettering, logos and transfers 21, 23, 25, 29, 91-93, 95, 102, 142-143
  silver 31, 138
  special/historic liveries 30-31, 41, 132, 138, 140, 143, 147-148, 150
Commercial Motor Show 7, 12, 18, 23, 138
Conductors 43-45, 78
Corporate contract work 134, 148
Corrosion 28, 87, 96, 116

Daily checks 107-108, 117
Dennis Dart 40-41
Deregulation 35, 37
Destination equipment 13, 16, 23, 47, 70, 82, 89, 91, 93, 101, 114, 127, 141
Differential 10, 19, 61, 99, 114-115, 120-121, 126
Dimensions 10, 12-13, 15, 20, 22-25, 38, 83, 103
Direction indicators 70-71, 93, 126, 128, 137, 151
Driver's cab 42, 70, 78-79, 95, 98, 101, 103, 114, 126
  control panel 98
  how to enter 101
  instruments and switches 71, 101, 112, 126
  periscope 101
  radio equipment 95
  seat 103, 114
Driving and handling 101
Durrant, A. A. M. 'Bill' 10

East London (Stagecoach) 32-33, 133
Eastern Coach Works 12, 16, 155
Electrical system 19, 35, 66-67, 87, 112, 125-127
  alternator 67, 90, 112, 125, 128
Emergency exits 23, 78, 81, 92, 98, 103, 114, 126, 141-142
Engine control systems 67-68
Engine cooling system 53-55, 106, 108, 111, 115-118
Engine lubrication system 52, 106-108, 114-115, 117, 125
  dipstick 107-108
  oil filters 125
Engines 10, 12, 32, 49-53, 75, 94, 98, 100-101, 155, 157
  AEC 11-12, 14, 19, 23-24, 43, 48-49, 68, 88, 90, 94, 106-107, 115, 118, 120, 125, 127, 142, 147, 151
  Cummins 39-41, 43-45, 83, 90, 99-100, 106, 116-120, 125, 127, 132, 135
  DAF 38
  Euro II 40- 41, 43, 45, 100, 132-135; III 132; V 100, 132
  Iveco 44, 90, 116, 118, 127, 143
  Leyland 15-17, 20-21, 25, 28, 30, 35-37, 40, 68, 90, 95, 106-107, 115, 118, 120, 127, 146, 148, 151

Scania 40, 90, 99, 106, 117, 125, 127, 136
Engine starting 108
Ensign Bus 37, 86, 135, 147
Exhaust system 56, 112, 118-119
Exports 7, 28, 32, 35-36, 40, 45, 86, 90, 136, 146, 154

Fares Fair programme 34-35
First London 44, 133, 138
Fleet numbers 27, 91, 93
Flooring 31, 42, 80, 98-99
Front entrance buses 23-24, 37, 72, 135, 137, 146
Fuel consumption 10, 30, 88, 94
Fuel system 55-56, 108, 112, 118, 128
  LPG 132, 152
Fuel tanks 13, 108, 112

Gangway slats 99, 114
Garage Showbuses 18, 91, 139, 146-147
Gearboxes 7, 12-14, 47, 57-58, 101, 103, 105, 118-120, 125-126
  AEC 19, 56
  Allison 42-43, 45, 100, 112, 119-120, 127, 132
  air-operated 11, 14, 19, 117
  checking oil 111, 119-120
  hydraulic 10-11, 14-16
  Wilson 100
Gear slip 119
Go Ahead London 43, 134
Green Line 12, 15-16, 22-23, 32, 121, 137, 141, 148, 151

Handbrake 11, 79, 103, 107, 114, 123-124, 128
Headlamps 16, 22, 33, 70, 79, 94, 108, 114, 128
Heritage routes (9 and 15) 7, 36, 44-45, 131-133, 138, 148
Heating system 7, 13-14, 20, 24, 47, 54, 71, 94, 98, 114, 118
Hydraulic system 11-12, 19, 59, 64-65, 89, 114, 117, 121

IM Vehicle 10-11
Insurance 89, 103

Jacking 107

Leyland 12, 15
  Atlantean 23
Lighting system 7, 22, 69-70, 87, 90, 93-94, 97, 108, 112, 128, 132
  fog light 70, 79, 93, 114, 126, 142
  interior 19, 22, 34, 69, 126, 128
  LED 135
Livingstone, Ken (Mayor of London) 40, 44-45
London Buses 32-34, 36, 39-40, 92, 132
London Central 40, 43, 136
London Coaches 38-39, 42
London Country 25-26, 29, 31-34, 43, 90, 140-142, 151
London Low Emission Zone (LEZ) 132, 153
London Northern 40
London Omnibus Traction Society (LOTS) 90
London Regional Transport 39, 92
London Transport – throughout
  50th anniversary 30-31
London Transport Museum 100, 142, 146, 150, 153
  Acton Depot 100, 137, 146, 150
  Covent Garden 30, 137, 146

London United 133
Low-floor buses 40, 44-45, 133, 136
Lubricants and fluids 106-107
  grease points 114
Luggage racks 16, 22, 33

Maintenance system 25-27, 37, 47-73, 95, 98, 115, 127
  engine changes 25
Metroline 133
MIRA test centre 13
Mirrors 79, 91-92, 103, 108, 114, 142
MoT 88-89, 103, 112, 114

National Bus Co. 28-29, 32, 141-142, 148, 151
Night blind 98
Non-passenger duties 32-33, 86, 90
Northern General 23-25, 28, 34, 90, 121-122, 143, 148, 151

One-person operation 23, 25, 28-30, 32-33, 35
Operation and maintenance manuals 100, 105, 118, 123, 125, 127
Open top buses 32-33, 37-39, 41-42, 133-135, 141

Painting 19-20, 26-27, 30, 34, 37, 82-83, 99, 102, 114
Park Royal Vehicles 11-13, 17-20, 22-24, 155
Platforms 7, 34, 77, 146
  doors 16-17, 22, 24, 33, 37-38, 41-43, 108, 114, 134-135, 141
  grab-rails 97, 132
Pre-production bus (RM8) 18, 41, 43-44, 49, 75, 94, 138, 147
Preserved railway operators 136
Private hire 45, 134, 147, 152
Privatisation 33, 37, 39-40, 92, 98, 151
Production figures 7, 17, 20-23, 30, 33, 93
Prototypes (RM1-RMC4) 11-13, 15-17, 20, 22, 44, 83, 90, 137, 143, 146, 150-151
Provincial bus museums 140, 147
Provincial and minor operators 36-37, 40, 134-135, 139-140, 147-148
PVS, Barnsley 40, 86, 88-89, 95, 100

Radiator/heat exchanger 12-14, 18, 54, 80, 111, 115, 117-118, 135
Radiator grille 13-16, 18-21, 23, 28-29, 80, 92, 135, 141, 148, 151
Railway replacement services 136
Rallies 85-86, 137, 139, 141, 143, 150
Rear-engined buses 24-25, 146
Refurbished RMs/RMLs 31, 39-40, 43, 45, 49, 55, 70, 78, 81, 83, 90, 93-95, 98, 119, 125-127, 132-133
Registrations 2, 23-24, 27, 36, 70, 89, 91-92, 9, 127, 141
Ride quality 12-13
Road tax 88, 103
Routemaster Association 90, 99-100, 107, 128
Routemaster 50th anniversary 43, 137, 143, 146, 148, 151-152
Route number display 16, 20, 70, 79, 82

Running costs 88, 103
Running days 44, 137-138, 140-141, 151

Safety 107
Scott, Douglas 11
Scottish operators 34-38, 41-42, 122, 133-135, 147-148
Scrapping 32, 34-36, 38, 40, 42-43, 86, 96, 148
Seating 7, 15-16, 34, 42, 82, 91, 93, 95, 97, 99, 127, 134, 142
  moquette upholstery 11, 16, 33, 42, 82, 93
Seating capacity 10, 12, 16, 22-25, 33, 38, 72
Sightseeing work 32-34, 37-39, 41-42, 133, 153
Single-deck buses 25, 30, 41, 152
Slave rigs 17
Spare parts 25, 29, 100, 127-128
Speed 94
Speedometer 71, 112, 121, 126
Staff and training buses 14, 32-33, 37
Stagecoach 37, 40, 43-44, 90, 133, 140, 153
Staircases 11, 23-24, 35, 69, 77-78, 114
  kick plates 99
Starter motor 68, 114, 125
Steering 7, 13-16, 19, 47, 60, 101, 112, 114, 120-121
Storage costs 88
Subframes 7, 11, 18, 25-27, 48-49, 75, 87, 111, 121, 128, 155
Suspension 7, 10, 12-14, 16, 19, 22, 24, 34, 47, 49, 60-61, 101, 112, 121

Tachograph 88-89, 103
Ticket bin 20, 78, 92
Tilt test 27
Tools and working facilities 107
Tow trucks 129
Trailer towing 23-24
Transmission – see also Gearboxes 14, 56-59, 111, 120-121
  fluid flywheel 53, 116, 118-119
  half-shafts 128-129
Transport for London 39-40, 43-45, 133
Trolleybus replacement 9, 11, 20-22

Valuations 89-90
Vehicle identities 26-27
Ventilation 13, 81, 103, 139
Video equipment 95

Watson, George 37
Websites and forums 90, 99-100, 107, 129
Wedding transport 134-135, 148
Weight 7, 10-14, 16, 20, 22-23, 25, 83
Weymann 12, 15, 155
Wheelchair lifts 38
Wheels and tyres 18, 20, 72, 82, 91, 94, 112, 121, 128, 151
Windows and windscreens 13, 19-20, 25, 45, 78, 81, 92, 98, 103, 108, 112, 114, 126-127, 132, 136-137, 139, 142, 151
Wings and headlamp panels 14-16, 18, 20, 23-24, 33, 79, 92, 114
  removing nearside wing 110
Withdrawals 15, 28, 32-33, 35, 37, 39, 43, 45, 90-91, 131, 146